Putting the Pieces Together

Ellis, Kim D.

    Putting the Pieces Together
Copyright © 2004, **aha!** Process, Inc., i-viii, 170 pp.
       Bibliography pp. 169-170
ISBN 1-929229-30-5

Putting the Pieces Together

Kim D. Ellis

Dedication

I thank God first for loving me and giving me the opportunity to speak to groups across the country about this important issue. When I began to think about dedicating this book, so many faces crossed my mind.

None of the book would have been written without the encouragement and insistence of my soul mate and husband of many years, David. My children, Kami, Aaron, and Jared, are a constant supply of love and support. It has not always been easy for them with their mother "on the road." To Mom and Dad, thanks for raising me with God-focused principles and ideals.

My life took a new and exciting turn when Dr. Ruby Payne entered my life. Thank you, Ruby, for opening my eyes to the needs and characteristics of the students I love to teach. Indeed, the activities in this book provide more examples of the ideas in *Learning Structures*, and grew out of your encouragement to continue to field test and collect them.

Thank you, Donna Magee, for being a constant sounding board and being so encouraging.

To the many teachers, administrators, and parents who have played such a vital role in the development of this book, and whose names are too numerous to mention, thank you.

Last, but certainly not least, my thanks go to the staff of **aha!** Process. My job would not be possible without your dedication and commitment to seeing the company run smoothly.

To our current teachers and those to come: May we continually look for new ways to reach, teach, and encourage all children.

Table of Contents

Cognitive Education
    Time 1
    Space 9
    Whole to Part/Part to Whole 17
    Labeling Processes 33
    Comparisons 39
    Label and Transfer 65

Incorporating Five Strategies into Instruction:
    Additional Activities for Modules 12-16 71

    Mental Models (Module 12) 71
    Planning to Control Impulsivity (Module 13) 89
    Plan and Label for Academic Tasks (Module 14) 99
    Question Making (Module 15) 131
    Sorting Strategies (Module 16) 145

Bibliography 169

Time

Along with a poor orientation of space, the absence of an internal referencing system caused by an unpredictable and fragmented environment can impair a child's ability to orient himself/herself in time. Children lacking internal referencing systems have difficulty fully comprehending a sequence of events. Information obtained can be distorted or fragmented. Students also will encounter problems with cause and effect, sequencing, and comparisons.

Time is a human-devised relationship between events or between other relationships.

The time that it takes to travel from Houston to Dallas or between any two locations is a relationship of speed and distance. Speed is the relationship between time and distance. Time is an abstract concept with no material existence. It is represented through material means such as a clock or watch. Children who have a poor orientation to time will work haphazardly and be unable to do things sequentially or with systematic exploration. The feelings of frustration and failure brought on by a test can cause students to hurry through instead of using the clock to their advantage to analyze, plan, and check their work. An equally problematic situation is when a child spends far too long on one particular question, not understanding the limits imposed by time.

Parents instill in their children the need for planning events from the time they are babies:

- "Time for a bath."
- "Time for dinner."
- "Pick up your toys before you go outside to play."

This creates a routine and instills in children an association between predictable actions and responses. If you pick up your toys, you will then be able to go outside. Visualizing the future is an important cognitive function, one of the basic abstractions children need to grasp. When a child comes to school without a basic understanding of time, teachers must mediate that weakness.

Understanding time is essential for completing assignments, sequencing, and accomplishing tasks. Students from generational poverty may not understand measured time. Time in poverty is generally perceived as the present. Many of our students do not have clocks at home. Students are woken up in the morning in a variety of ways, including even by the arrival of the school bus. Do you have students who are continuously tardy?

One young teacher recounted to me the following story:

When she was 17, her family adopted two young children, ages 6 and 9. One particular morning the mother was leaving early for an appointment with a doctor in a nearby city. The "wake-up call" was going to be the responsibility of the 17-year-old. As she talked to the children the night before, she let them know she would be waking them up. The 9-year-old replied, "Don't worry, because I know how to get up on my own. Before I got here, I had to wake up for the bus each morning. All ya gotta do is drink two big glasses of water before you go to bed, and a little before the bus comes ya gotta get up and go!" For four years, the child had followed the same routine, except on weekends, so that he wouldn't miss the bus.

When his new older sister questioned the importance of not missing the bus, he informed her that they would do without breakfast if they didn't make it to school on time.

Direct-teaching of elapsed time is needed. Tightly structured lessons in which time frames are established will help children. Students can be asked to sketch their visualization of time. Student responses vary greatly but are enlightening. One teacher explained to her class that time moved throughout the day in relation to the activities and content areas they were scheduled to encounter. Each activity or subject area was placed next to a time on a timeline that had been put on the board. As the day progressed, activity and content cards went up on the board (see page 5). The areas that were constant remained in place each day, while the activities that varied were moved accordingly. A few weeks after the line had been put up, one of the teacher's fourth-graders asked why the time line was top-to-bottom. He said, "Time doesn't move that way."

When the teacher asked for an explanation, he said, "The sun comes up in the morning, then it's noon, and then the sun starts down. It would make more sense if the line went across the bottom." While he spoke, the young man moved his hand from left to right. The class agreed to leave both lines on the board. The vertical line was used as the primary line, but throughout the course of the day, the teacher would have a student move an activity or content area to the horizontal line. She also spent a portion of each day questioning the students about time, as in:

- "What happened just before math?"
- "Where will we be in one hour?"

Another example for younger students can be found on page 7. It is a schedule web that was used to illustrate the events and subjects areas for the day.

Step sheets, which are discussed in additional activities for Module 13, are very beneficial to a child with a poor concept of time. Teachers who work with younger students need to reinforce throughout the day steps in relation to time.

Statements such as these can be used:

- "After you return to your seat."
- "Before you sit down."
- "In the next five minutes."

Timers can be used to create a sense of distance between the beginning and the end of an assignment. The task can be broken into segments and each segment set against a time frame. One example would be to use rote math drills against a set amount of time. Students grade for accuracy during each particular time frame. The time frame can gradually be reduced to create an increased awareness. Students enjoy this activity when they're being graded against themselves and not others. Students graph their scores and monitor their progress. A middle school teacher from Maryland began to use three-minute egg timers with her students so they could monitor their time spent working math problems. The students were so fascinated by the sand that they discussed the concept of "moving time" for an entire class period. The timers were not intended as a pacing guide but as a means of gauging time spent on easier and more difficult problems. If the same amount of time was spent with both types of problems, adjustments needed to be made.

Many high school students have trouble scheduling work, homework, sleep, friends, etc. A high school teacher in Texas helped students by creating a timeline of events, beginning with waking up and ending with going to sleep (as illustrated on page 6). Students were able to see the realities of the time that they actually had to work with during the course of the day.

The activities on the following pages can be used to help students with their understanding of time.

Purpose: To establish a daily understanding of elapsed time during the school day.
Materials: Wall chart and sentence strips or white/chalk board and markers.
Vocabulary: Time, numbers, hour, minutes, elapsed, between, until, before, after.

Activity 1: How Do You See Time? page 5

1. Create a chart of the basic time frames involved in the class. Amount of time will vary depending on the schedule.
2. Place sentence strips containing the content area or activity related to the beginning time.
3. Question students throughout the day concerning elapsed time between subject areas and activities.
4. Discuss vocabulary related to the timeline: before, after, next, following, between.

Variations:

1. Selected activities can be placed on a horizontal line to express the idea of time differently.
2. Secondary teachers use a 45- to 90-minute time frame instead of the full day.

Activity 2: Plan the School Day, page 6

1. Students label activities on the timeline from wake-up until bedtime. Specific times are listed for school, work, homework, and other appropriate activities. Students establish their own schedules.

Activity 3: Schedule Web, page 7

1. To aid younger students, colored markers are placed on the activity at the beginning of each time period. Teachers suggest using a white board with laminated content areas and activities. Magnets are placed on the backs of each activity to make movement easier to facilitate. Special-event markers are used for assemblies, field trips, and special occasions.

Time

How do you see time?

8:00
8:30
9:00
9:30
10:00
10:30
11:00
11:30
12:00　Lunch
12:30
1:00
1:30
2:00
2:30
3:00

8:00　9:00　10:00　11:00　12:00　1:00　2:00　3:00

HS level

Plan the School Day

6:00 a.m.	6:30
7:00	7:30
	8:30
	9:30
	10:30
	11:30 Lunch
12:00 Noon	
1:00	
2:00	
3:00	
4:00	4:30
5:00	5:30
6:00	6:30
7:00	7:30
8:00	8:30
9:00	9:30
10:00	10:30
11:00	

www.ahaprocess.com

Schedule Web

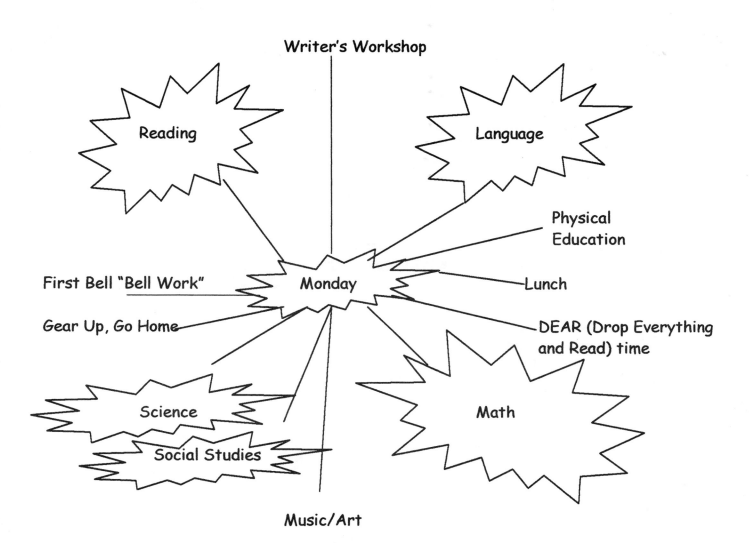

Writer's Workshop

Reading

Language

Physical Education

First Bell "Bell Work"

Monday

Lunch

Gear Up, Go Home

DEAR (Drop Everything and Read) time

Science

Math

Social Studies

Music/Art

Cognitive Strategies

To control impulsivity teach str. #1,4,5,7-10

comes from birth to 5yrs old

INPUT:
quantity and
quality of
data gathered

go together

see p.9
R/L front
back, etc.

1. Use planning behaviors. *create; to follow plan must have formal register*
2. Focus perception on specific stimulus.
3. Control impulsivity. *hurrying; incomplete tasks*
4. Explore data systematically.
5. Use appropriate and accurate labels. *vocabulary*
6. Organize space using stable systems of reference.
7. Orient data in time.
8. Identify constancies across variations. *be able to sort*
9. Gather precise and accurate data.
10. Consider two sources of information at once.
11. Organize data (parts of a whole).
12. Visually transport data.

1. Identify and define the problem.
2. Select relevant cues.
3. Compare data.
4. Select appropriate categories of time.
5. Summarize data.
6. Project relationships of data.
7. Use logical data.
8. Test hypothesis.
9. Build inferences.
10. Make a plan using the data.
11. Use appropriate labels.
12. Use data systematically.

ELABORATION:
efficient use of
the data

OUTPUT:
communication
of elaboration
and input

1. Communicate clearly the labels and process.
2. Visually transport data correctly.
3. Use precise and accurate language.
4. Control impulsive behavior.

Adapted from the work of Reuven Feuerstein — *worked w/kids between ages 11-15 yr. olds*

helped explain why kids fail in school (in the classroom)

www.ahaprocess.com

Space

As teachers, we have assumed that students understand common directions, such as left, right, over, under, front, below, top, and back. Orienting space can be loosely characterized by direction. Space can extend in all directions horizontally. When vertical dimension is added, it becomes three-dimensional space. Space can also refer to distance and location. Many students, however, have a very difficult time with directionality because they have not developed an internal referencing system for space. Poor spatial reference exhibits itself in many ways in the classroom. Students will have a difficult time following and giving directions, locating events in context, and understanding and analyzing situations. Many students cannot picture themselves in another's shoes. The only perspective they can acquaint themselves with is their own. Students cannot locate a concrete object and change the orientation in their mind, which is the basis of cognitive development needed to handle "What if?" types of hypothetical situations and thinking.

On page 14 students are asked to diagram their classroom. A transparency should be used by the teacher to direct the process. Start with the door nearest to the teacher's desk. Students and the teacher will then make appropriate drawings and label each item as they move around the perimeter of the room. Once the perimeter is complete, move to the interior of the room and include all desks and tables in the drawing. After the drawing is complete, divide the students into two groups. A final destination for the teacher will be given, but each group will have a different starting point. The group will write directions to move the teacher from the starting point to the destination. The destination is the same, but the directions must be different in order to reach the destination. If the directions are written correctly, that will occur. If not, laughter is usually the result, along with an important lesson in accuracy, clarity, and direction. Many teachers continue to use the drawing on a regular basis to reinforce the concepts of directionality in the classroom. The students can practice changes in orientation by describing the location of various concrete objects in relation to themselves and others in the classroom. Question examples are listed on page 11.

The room activities and arrow/directionality activities on pages 12 and 13 seek to give children an internal reference system with which they can control space by teaching them to discern, organize, articulate, and abstractly represent spatial arrangements.

Organization of Space

Students could have difficulty in the following areas if they cannot orient space and understand abstract time:

READING

Before, prefixes
After, suffixes
"In the beginning ... "
Sequencing
Author's point of view

WRITING

Descriptive space/order words: first, next, then, etc.
Sequence of steps of a task
Point of view
Writing in third person
Proper placement of punctuation marks

MATH

Place value
Greater than and less than
Definition of field
"Joe is taller than Fred but shorter than Bill"
Probability and outcomes

10

Purpose: To develop a mental model for space.
Materials: Pencil and pages 12-14.
Vocabulary: Right, left, front, behind, dot, arrow.

Activity 1: Orientation of Space

1. Students stand at their desks and hold a pencil with the eraser touching their nose, lead ends pointing directly in front of them.
2. Students name the person to their right and to their left.
3. Students make a 180° turn.
4. Repeat question.
5. Discuss why the answers changed.

Activity 2: Arrows, pages 12-13

1. Read the directions together, labeling the key words.
2. Review key vocabulary.
3. Mark the first row with the students on overhead, modeling the correct answers.
4. Students complete the page independently without turning the paper.
5. Check.

Activity 3: Draw the Classroom, page 14

1. Make transparency and individual student copies of the blank classroom page.
2. Students label the room on paper while the teacher models on the overhead the location of objects, doors, desks, windows, chalkboards, etc., in the room. See example on page 15.
3. Students work with a partner to write directions for moving individuals from their desk to different parts of the room.
4. Students must include right, left, front, back, and other appropriate words with the number of steps to be taken to reach the designated area. Example: Student 1C to the bookcase, 5B to the teacher's desk, 4B to the computer, and 3A to teacher's desk, then to the outside door.

Draw a large dot on the side of the point of the arrow that is indicated by left, right, front, or behind in each box. Do not turn your paper as you work.

RIGHT	LEFT	FRONT	BEHIND	RIGHT
FRONT	RIGHT	BEHIND	LEFT	FRONT
BEHIND	RIGHT	LEFT	FRONT	RIGHT
LEFT	BEHIND	RIGHT	FRONT	RIGHT
BEHIND	FRONT	LEFT	RIGHT	LEFT

Look carefully at each box. If a direction is given, draw a large dot on the side indicated.
If a dot is shown, write the direction in relation to the tip of the arrow. Do not turn your
paper as you work.

⬅ (dot top-left) ___	⬇ BEHIND	➡ (dot top-left) ___	⬆ FRONT
⬆ (dot left) ___	➡ (dot top) ___	⬅ LEFT	⬇ (dot bottom) ___
⬅ RIGHT	⬇ (dot top) ___	⬆ (dot top) ___	⬅ LEFT
⬅ (dot bottom-left) ___	⬆ LEFT	⬅ (dot top) ___	⬇ BEHIND

Draw the Classroom

Classroom

Notes

Whole to Part/Part to Whole

Students must understand the concept of part to whole to be able organize data.

In order to understand and label part to whole, students must be able to explore data systematically, see constancies across variations, organize space, and understand the labeling process.

We begin by directly teaching how the whole can be divided into parts and labeled with:

- Numbers.
- Letters.
- Colors.
- Symbols.

Workbook pages 19 and 20 give an example of how students can use shaped blocks to work with whole to part. The student chooses a shape to trace on his/her paper. Students are given the number of parts that their shape is to be divided into. Once the shape has been traced and divided, the student then labels the parts with a number, letter, color, or symbol.

Students learn to create and label a new image by using three separate shapes. Pages 21 and 22 give an example of how one student used the three shapes to create a new image. Many younger students have difficulty with the labeling process because they continue to see separate shapes instead of individual sections. Students are encouraged to trace around the outside of the new image with a dark crayon or marker before they begin to label.

Students who don't have a concrete understanding of part to whole and whole to part will face many challenges in the classroom. Sentence structure is difficult to understand, as is paragraph construction. In order to understand the scientific process, students must first be able to organize information. Without an understanding of part/whole concepts, the task is very difficult to accomplish. An understanding of historical events requires an understanding of time, space, and part to whole.

The following activities were used to help students create a mental model for part to whole.

Purpose: To develop a mental model for whole to part and part to whole.
Materials: Pencil, wooden or plastic shape blocks and 19, 21, 24, 26, 28, 30.
Vocabulary: Corners, sides, intersection, point, segment, ray, part, whole.

Activity 1: Whole to Part, page 19

1. Students are asked to define what they see on the page.
   - How many segments?
   - How many corners?
   - How many points of intersection?
2. Students label the corners of each shape.
3. Read and label the directions.
4. Students label the final product.

Activity 2: Part to Whole, page 21

1. Students choose or are given three plastic or wooden shape pieces. Paper examples at the bottom of the page can be used if plastic or wooden pieces are not available.
2. Students create a new image using the three shapes.
3. The image is repeated in the second box.
4. Students label the image by numbering each section.
5. Students label the image by coloring each section.

the word ~~issue~~ *equal* is not in directions

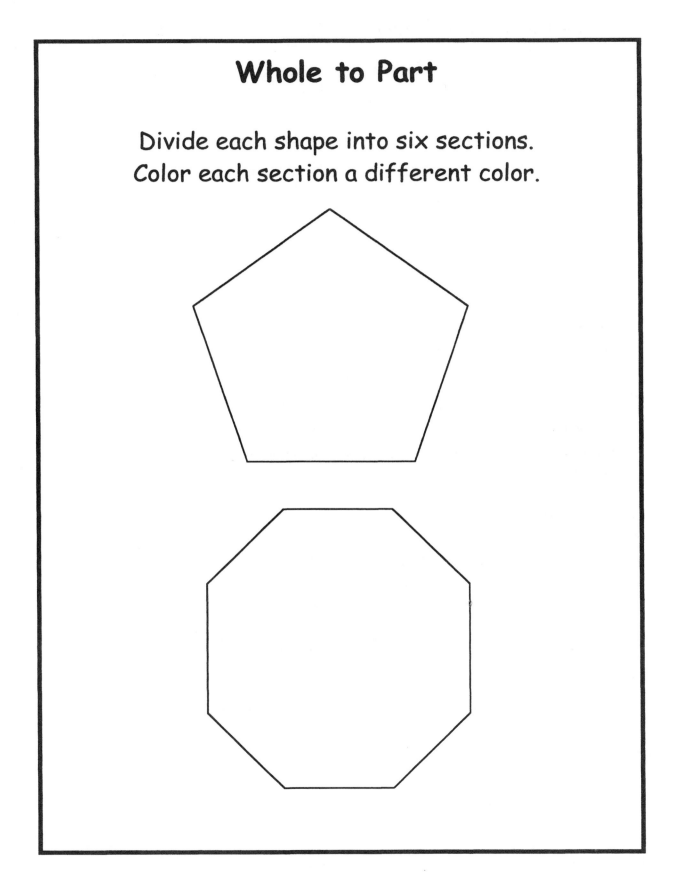

Whole to Part

Divide each shape into six sections.
Color each section a different color.

Whole to Part

Divide each shape into six sections.
Color each section a different color.

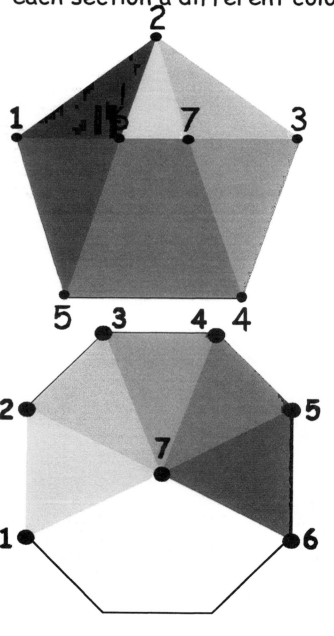

Part to Whole

Using three shapes, create a new image in the box below. Repeat the image in the second box.

After the new image is created, number each section differently.

After the new image is created, color each section a different color.

Part to Whole

Using three shapes, create a new image in the box below. Repeat the image in the second box.

After the new image is created, color each section a different color.

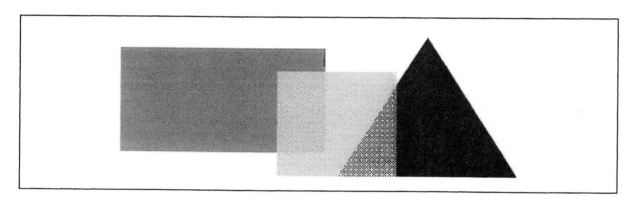

After the new image is created, number each section differently.

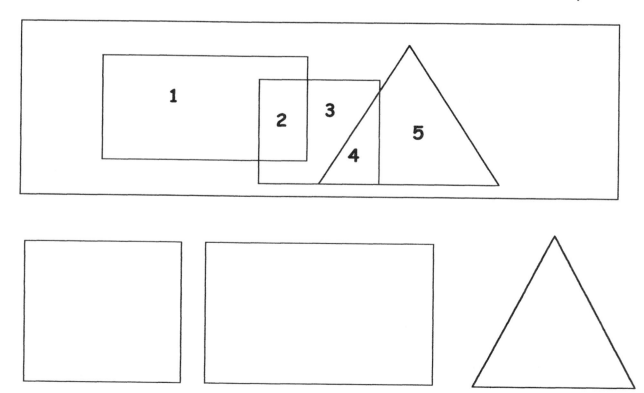

www.ahaprocess.com

Activity 3: page 24

1. Students define what they see on the page.
2. Students label the key words in the directions.
3. Markers or crayons can be used to label the first image with color.
4. The second image on each row is to be labeled with numbers.

Answers will vary, but the total number of sections will remain the same.

Activities 4-6: pages 26, 28, 30

1. Students define what they see on each page.
2. The model in the upper right hand corner is labeled with numbers at each point of intersection.
3. Students label each of the line segments in Column 1 and Column 2.
4. Using the completed model in the upper right-hand corner as a frame of reference, students determine which two sets of segments will create the whole.
5. Students write the letter of a box from Column 2 containing the missing segments they have chosen to create the whole next to the numbers 1-5.

In the figures below, different shapes are used to create a new picture.

Color each section a different color.   Place a number in each section.

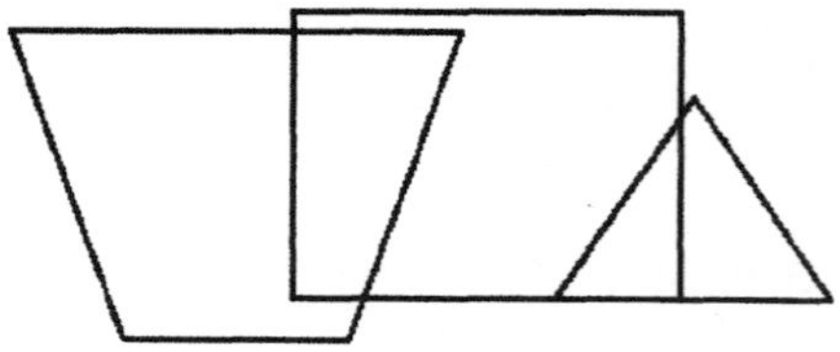

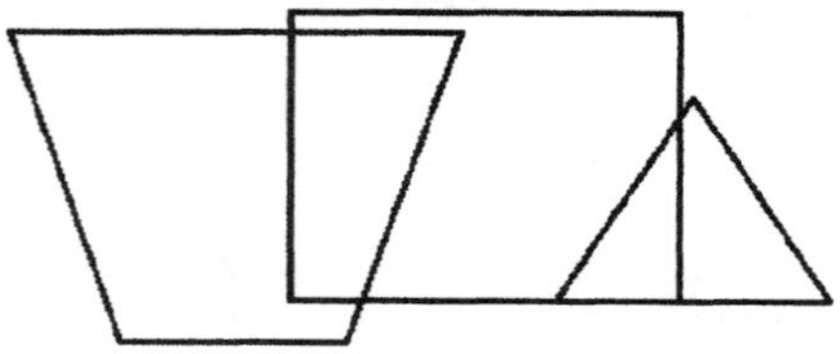

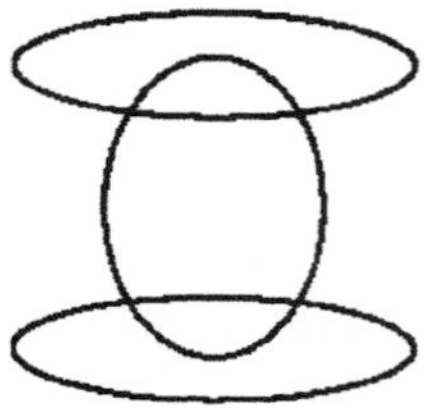

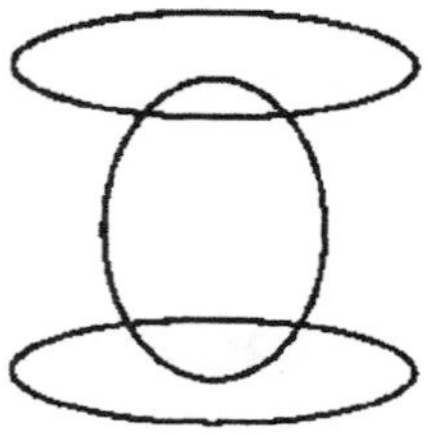

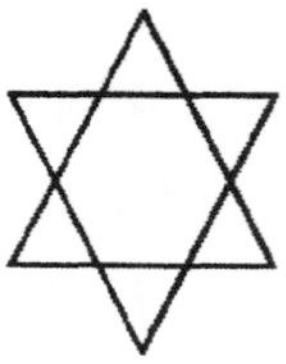

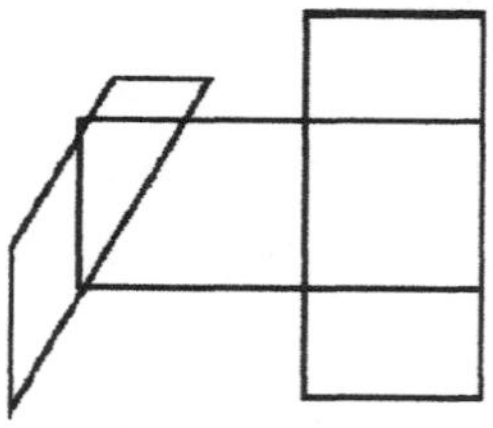

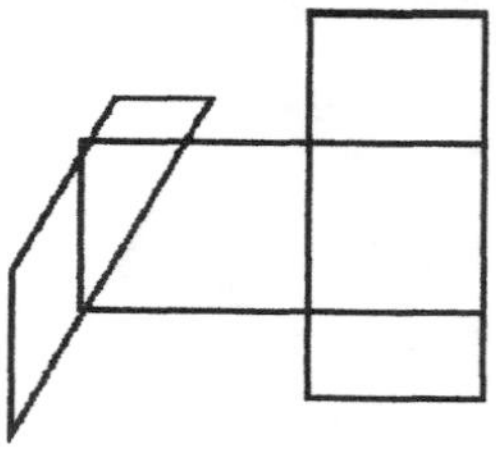

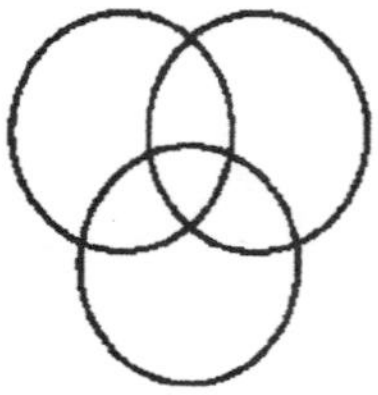

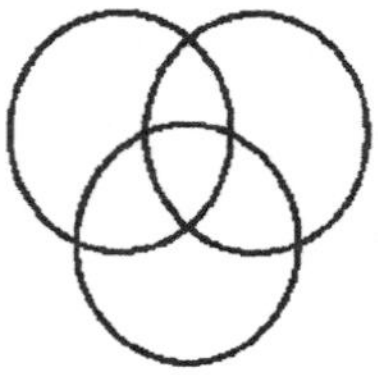

www.ahaprocess.com

In the figures below, different shapes are used to create a new picture.

Color each section a different color.   Place a number in each section.

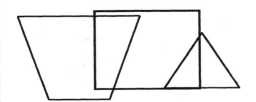   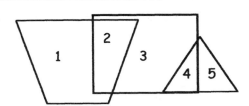

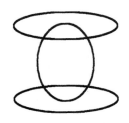   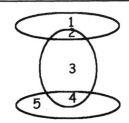

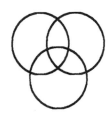   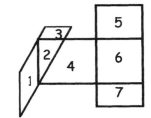

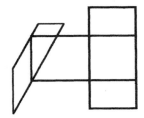   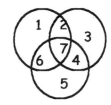

NAME_____

Take a figure from Column 1 and combine it
with a figure from Column 2 to make the
shape to the right of this information. Put
the number and letter that create the
original shape on the line in the middle.

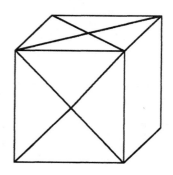

Column 1

Column 2

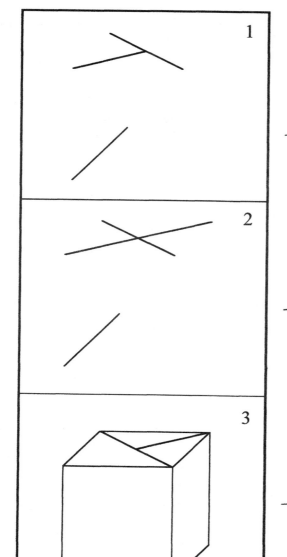

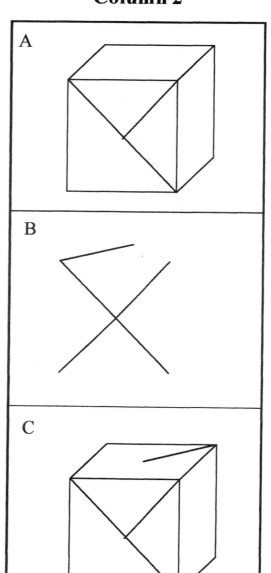

NAME _____

Take a figure from Column 1 and combine it with a figure from Column 2 to make the shape to the right of this information. Put the number and letter that create the original shape on the line in the middle.

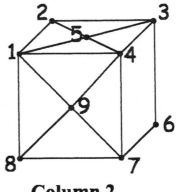

Column 1   Column 2

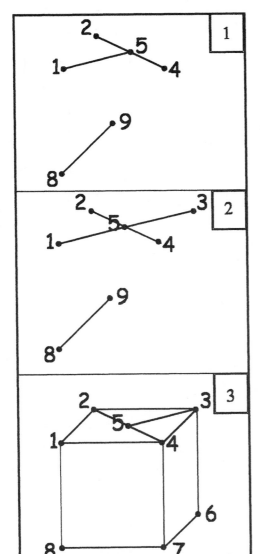

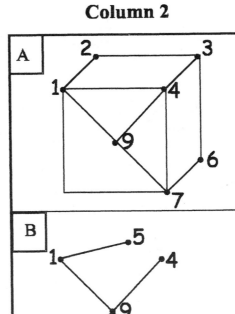

NAME _____

Take a figure from Column 1 and combine
it with a figure from Column 2 to make
the shape to the right of this information.
Put the number and letter that create the
original shape on the line in the middle.

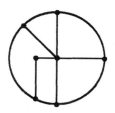

Column 1

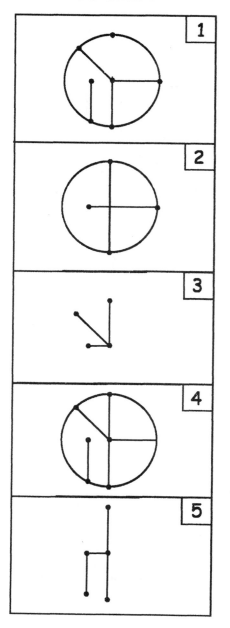

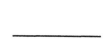

Column 2

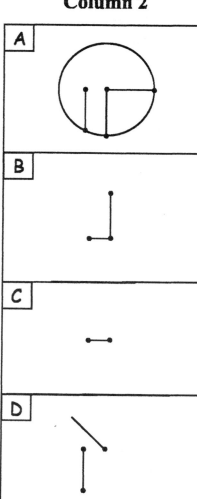

NAME _____

Take a figure from Column 1 and combine
it with a figure from Column 2 to make
the shape to the right of this information.
Put the number and letter that create the
original shape on the line in the middle.

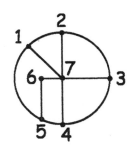

Column 1

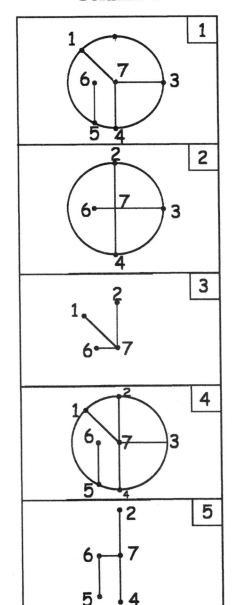

Column 2

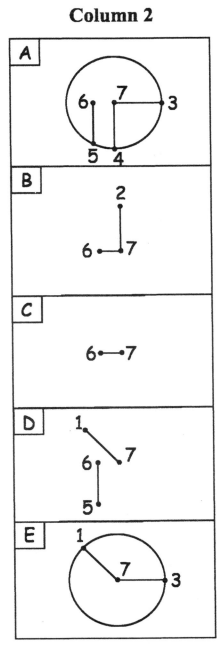

1B _____

2D _____

3A _____

4C _____

5E _____

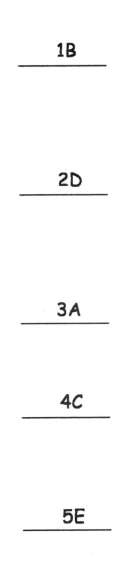

NAME _____

Take a figure from Column 1 and combine
it with a figure from Column 2 to make
the shape to the right of this information.
Put the number and letter that create the
original shape on the line in the middle.

Column 1

Column 2

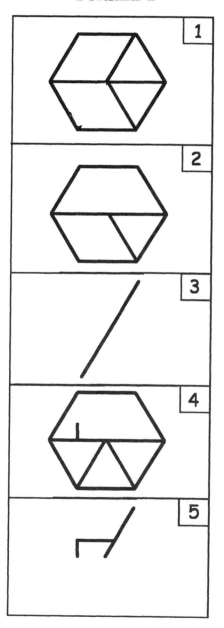

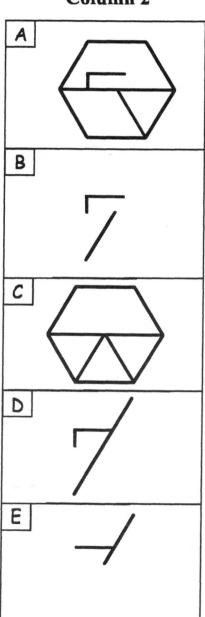

www.ahaprocess.com

NAME _____

Take a figure from Column 1 and combine
it with a figure from Column 2 to make
the shape to the right of this information.
Put the number and letter that create the
original shape on the line in the middle.

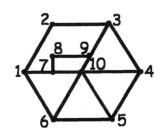

Column 1

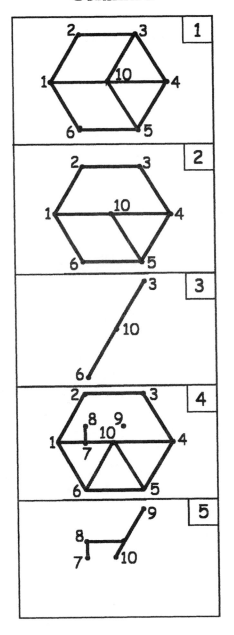

Column 2

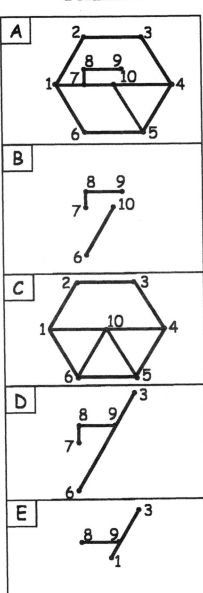

1B

2D

3A

4E

5C

Notes

Labeling Processes

Before being introduced to labeling processes and the reasoning behind them, students must understand the differences in convergent thinking. Doctors, technicians, nurses, and emergency medical personnel are frequently called upon for quick medical decisions that require a clear understanding of the problems, best possible solutions, medicines, and treatments available. Determining what you are going to do on Saturday night simply involves reflecting and considering alternatives. Generating ideas and planning both require seeing in one's mind how something might look before one attempts it. Daydreaming is a form of imagining that involves hypothetical thinking and representation. Anticipation involves thoughts about looking forward to the outcome of an event or action. Drawing conclusions based on the facts: When you put 5 and 5 together you get 10.

Processing information in order to find a solution to a problem or an adequate response to a question depends on taking the time to gather necessary and specific information, to elaborate it properly, and to communicate the answer thoroughly, clearly, and concisely.

In order to develop a plan, students must be able to gather, use, and express data. In order to gather data, students must follow seven basic steps:

1. Gather clear and complete information.
2. Use a plan or system so that we don't miss or skip information.
3. Label our findings so that we can remember and articulate them clearly.
4. Describe things in terms of when and where they occur.
5. Determine characteristics that stay the same.
6. Organize the information by considering more than one characteristic at a time.
7. Be precise and accurate.

Students must be taught the individual steps of the process, what each one means, and examples of how they are used. We must organize information and thoughts to create order, save time, be more efficient, focus our attention, and understand the connection between objects, words, and characteristics.

The basic elements of a plan include:
- Defining objectives — what we hope to accomplish.
- Taking note of the information we have — what has been given.
- Planning a specific strategy.
- Deciding on a starting point.
- Determining the rules and parameters that govern our activities.
- Devising a way to check our work.

The activities and examples on pages 35-38 help to reinforce the concepts involved in planning without using content examples. Students work with shapes, designs, and diamonds instead of words. The purpose is to directly teach the steps required in gathering and utilizing data, identifying characteristics, organizing thoughts, and planning the work.

The activities will challenge students to gather information, organize their thoughts, plan, put the plan to work, and adjust as needed to complete the task.

Purpose: To directly teach the steps required in gathering and utilizing data, organizing thoughts, and planning the work.
Materials: Pencil and pages 35, 37.
Vocabulary: Copy, label, corners, intersection.

Activity: Visual Transfer with Labeling

1. Students define and discuss what they see on the page. Teacher-directed discussion should focus on the plan needed to copy the design.
2. Students develop a plan, which should include determining a starting point, labeling the points of intersection, and defining and labeling area markers.
3. Sample questions to prompt student discussion: How far is the design from the left/right of the box? What is the distance from the left side of the design to the right? What is the distance from the top to the bottom of the design?
4. Students label beginning points.
5. Students measure and mark distance from the right/left and top/bottom.
6. Students copy the design.

Look at the design on the left. Copy the design in the next frame.

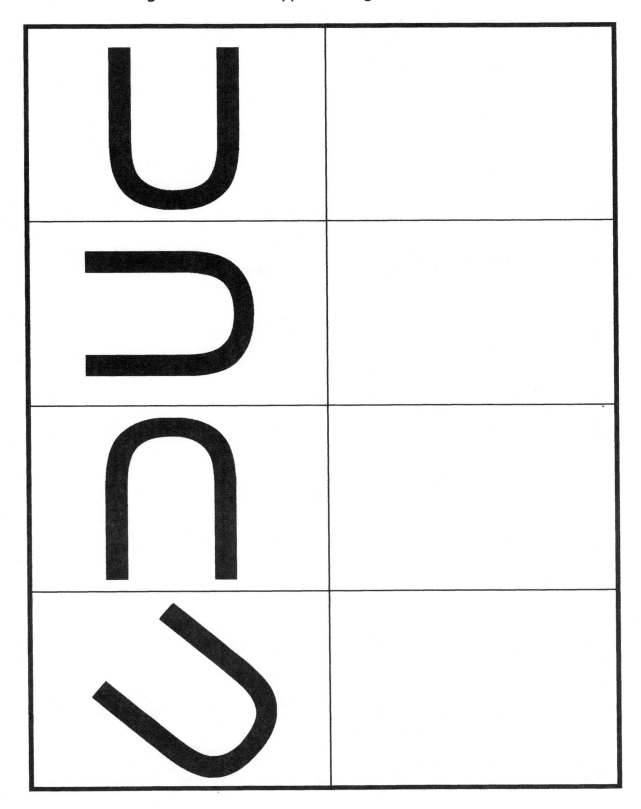

Look at the design on the left. Copy the design in the next frame.

1 2　　3 4 (letter U)	1 2　　3 4
1 2 / 3 4 (letter C shape)	1 / 2 / 3 / 4
1 2　3 4 (inverted U)	1 2　3 4
3 4 / 1 2 (rotated U)	3 4 / 1 2

Look at the design on the left. Copy the design in the next frame.

Look at the design on the left. Copy the design in the next frame.

Comparisons

Basic to all cognitive processes is the ability to compare. It is through comparison that we organize and sort bits and pieces of information into coordinated and organized pieces of thought. As we receive new information,

we organize,

    compare,

        sort,

           and classify

against information that has already been stored. We can only integrate the new information with the old if we find relationships between them.

Our intention is to develop comparative behavior in students. When students don't have the ability to sort characteristics, information, and events, these become isolated, separate, one-time experiences. Many times students don't have the verbal tools to express their ideas, comparisons, and findings.

Additionally, more problems arise if students don't use the same parameters for comparison. For instance, that fish have gills and cats have fur are facts, but these facts don't form an accurate comparison. In order to compare, using the same parameters, we would say fish breathe through gills and cats breathe with lungs. An accurate comparison requires that objects be subjected to the same criteria. In order to compare, we must find what items share and where and how they're different. An individual must be able to compare two or more objects and traits. Students must also be able to judge, classify, and establish relationships in order to form comparisons.

The following activities can be used to help students identify specific characteristics and constancies across variations, visually transfer, work systematically, make the indicated changes, and label their work.

Purpose: To identify and change specific characteristics.
Materials: Pencil, markers or crayons, and pages 41-46.
Vocabulary: Number, color, size, form, frame, sample.

Activity: Identifying Characteristics, page 41

1. Students discuss and define what they see on the page.
2. Students label the directions. Key words — only the changes indicated.
3. Activity will work better if a transparency of the page is used by the teacher to model how to work the page.
4. The first two rows on page 41 should be worked together before students complete the remainder of the page.

Look at the sample. In each of the two frames, make a new drawing using **only** the changes indicated.

△	number color size form	number color size form
○○○	number color size form	number color size form
↑	number color size form	number color size form
◇◇	number color size form	number color size form
□□ □	number color size form	number color size form
⬡	number color size form	number color size form

Look at the sample. In each of the two frames, make a new drawing using only the changes indicated.

△	(number) color size form	number (color) size form
○ ○ ○	number color (size) form	number color size (form)
↑	(number) color (size) form	number (color) size (form)
◇ ◇	(number) color (size) form	number (color) (size) form
□ □ □	(number) color size (form)	(number) (color) size form
⬡	number (color) (size) form	number color (size) (form)

Look at the sample. In each of the two frames, make a new drawing using **only** the changes indicated.

(triangle)	number (color) size form	number color (size) form
(three circles)	number color size (form)	number color (size) form
(arrow)	(number) color size (form)	number (color) (size) form
(two diamonds)	number (color) size (form)	(number) color size (form)
(three squares)	(number) (color) size form	(number) color (size) form
(octagon)	(number) color (size) form	number (color) size (form)

Look at the sample. In each of the two frames, make a new drawing using **only** the changes indicated.

△	number color (size) form	number color size (form)
○ ○ ○	number color size (form)	(number) color size form
↑	number (color) size (form)	(number) color (size) form
◇ ◇	(number) (color) size form	(number) (color) size form
□ □ □	number (color) size (form)	number (color) (size) form
⬡	(number) color size (form)	(number) color size (form)

Look at the sample. In each of the two frames, make a new drawing using **only** the changes indicated.

△	number color size (form)	(number) color size form
○ ○ ○	(number) color size form	number (color) size form
↑	(number)(color) size form	(number)(color) size form
◇ ◇	number (color)(size) form	number (color)(size) form
☐ ☐ ☐	number (color)(size) form	(number) color size (form)
⬡	number (color) size (form)	number (color)(size) form

Look at the sample. In each of the two frames, make a new drawing using **only** the changes indicated.

	number color size (form)	(number) color size form
	number (color) size form	(number) color size form
	number (color) (size) form	number color (size) (form)
	(number) color size (form)	number (color) size (form)
	(number) color (size) form	number (color) size (form)
	number color (size) (form)	number (color) size form

Purpose: To identify and adapt specific characteristics.

Materials: Pencil and page 48.

Vocabulary: Shape, square, circle, hexagon, lightning bolt, arrow, diamond, cross, pentagon, top, bottom, inside, horizontal, vertical, congruent.

Activity: Adapting Characteristics, page 48

1. Students are asked to study the page for one minute, then turn the paper over.
2. The teacher asks students to give the directions for the page.
3. The discussion needs to focus on the vocabulary required to accomplish the task.
4. The students are to copy, in the second frame, a drawing that will duplicate the same characteristics as in the first frame, using the new shape. An example is found on page 49.

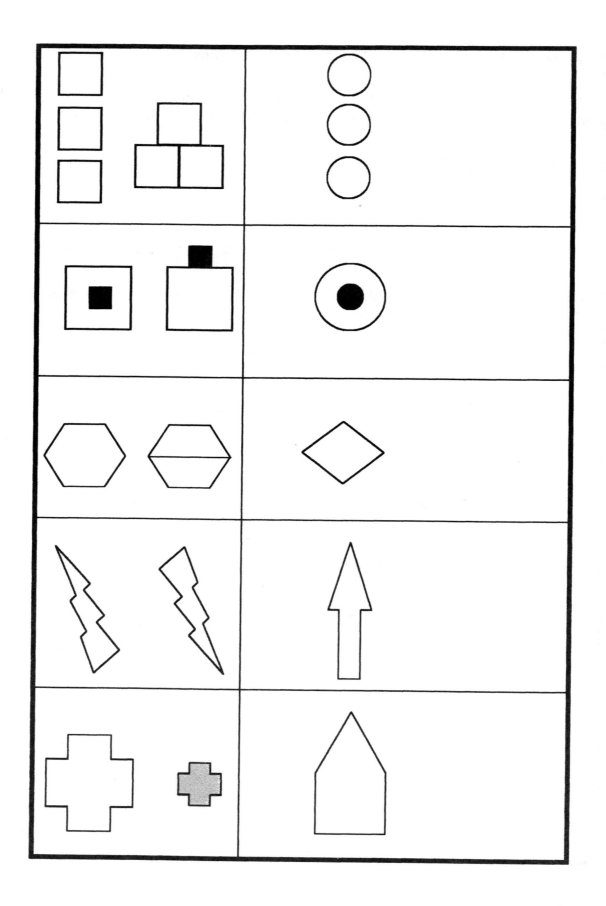

www.ahaprocess.com

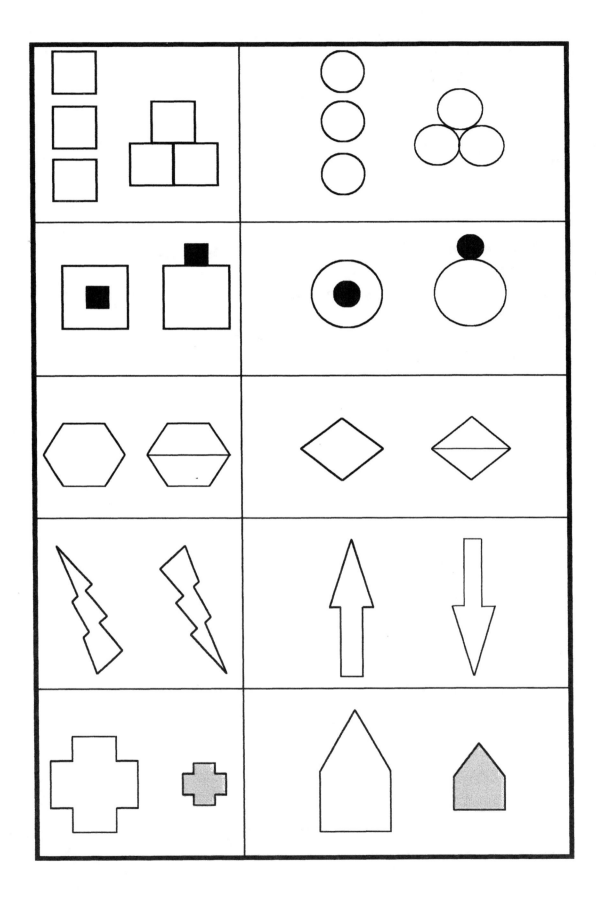

Purpose: To use planning and labeling to solve a task.
Materials: Pencil and pages 51-58.
Vocabulary: Shape, corners, sides, angle, congruent, triangle, square, symmetrical, asymmetrical.

Activity: Dots, pages 51-58

1. Students must identify the problem. (Connect the dots to make the figures like the one in the model.)
2. Students must develop a plan of how to accomplish the task. (Where will you begin? Where is a good place to start?)
3. Students must identify a labeling system to use with the task. (Will you label with numbers or letters?)
4. Students must work systematically through the plan.
5. Students must evaluate their work.
6. On some pages the students must identify the error. (What must change for the task to be completed correctly?)

Look at the model on the left. Decide which dots can be connected to match the model. The new shapes must be the exact size and shape as the model.

Look at the model on the left. Decide which dots can be connected to match the model. The new shapes must be the exact size and shape as the model.

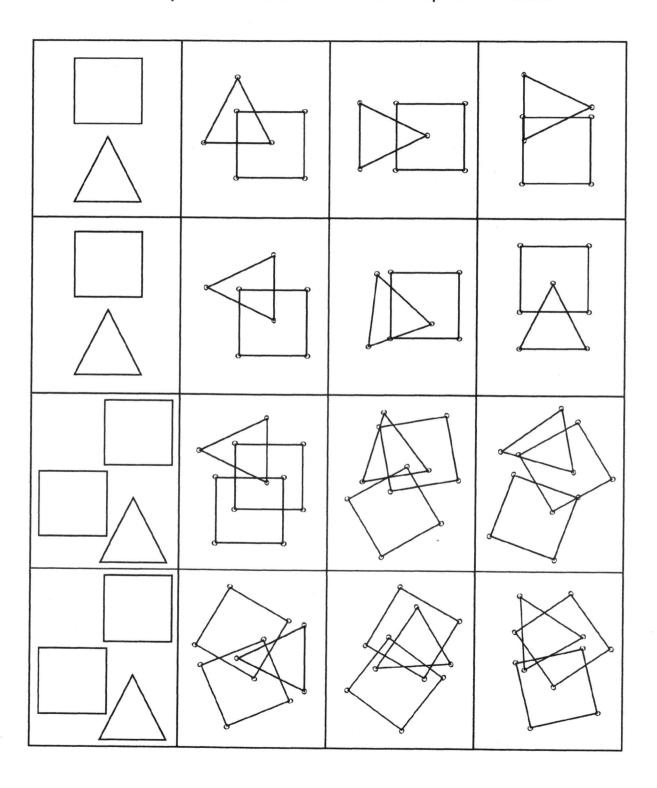

www.ahaprocess.com

Look at the model on the left. Decide which dots can be connected to match the model. The new shapes must be the exact size and shape as the model.

Look at the model on the left. Decide which dots can be connected to match the model. The new shapes must be the exact size and shape as the model.

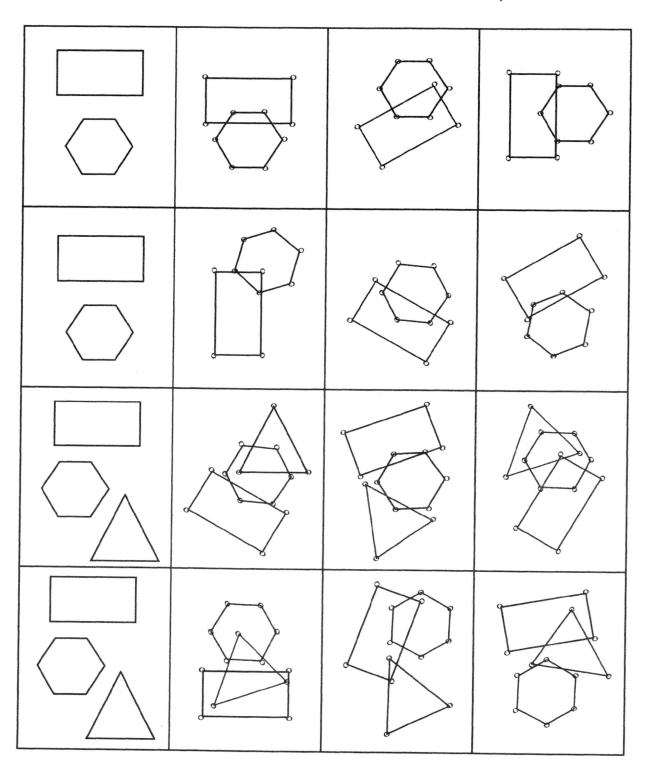

www.ahaprocess.com

Look at the model on the left. Decide which dots can be connected to match the model. Identify any errors with the following codes: a = extra dot, b = dot missing, c = dot in wrong place, d = no mistake.

Error_____   Error_____   Error_____

Error_____   Error_____   Error_____

Look at the model on the left. Decide which dots can be connected to match the model. Identify any errors with the following codes: a = extra dot, b = dot missing, c = dot in wrong place, d = no mistake.

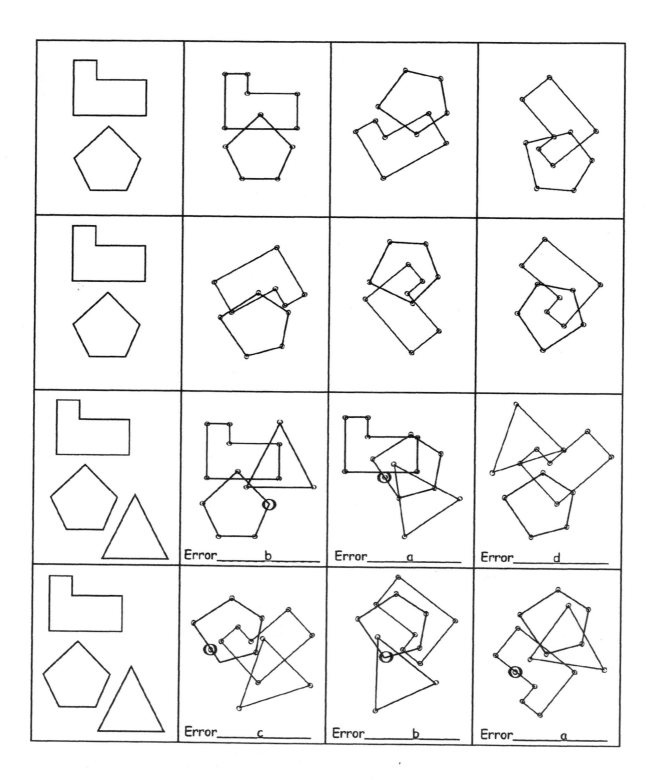

56   www.ahaprocess.com

ORGANIZATION OF SPACE: Look at the models.
Connect the dots to re-create the models.

1

2

3

4

3

1

4

2

5

3

aha! Process, Inc.

Orientation changes
- What do you do 1st? Connect open diamonds in #1, 2; in box #3 - 5 look for
pt. 1-4 to find that shape

**ORGANIZATION OF SPACE: Look at the models.
Connect the dots to re-create the models.**

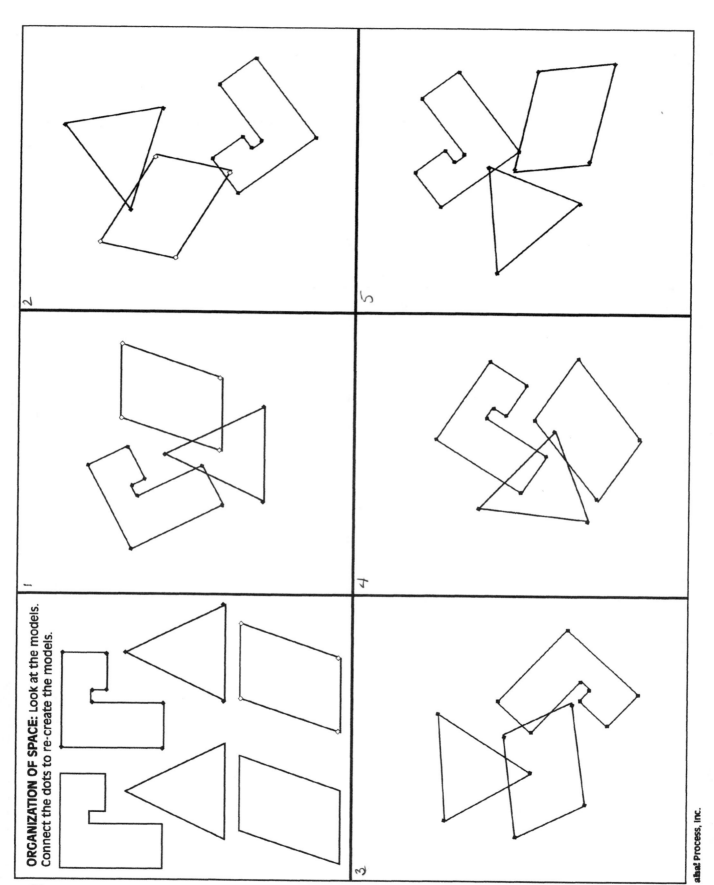

58   www.aha process.com

Purpose: To understand orientation of space.
Materials: Pencil, scissors and pages 60-63.

Activity: Creating dot transfer pages, pages 60-63

Students can use a blank grid to create a dots page of their own. Use small wood or plastic shape pieces. Students then trace the shapes in the left column in box 1A. Move the two shapes to box 1B (second column), change the orientation, and place a dot on each corner of the shape. Move the two shapes to 1C (third column), change the orientation, and repeat. When the students have completed their pages, they can trade papers and find the answers on the other students' grids. The students need to develop a plan for finding the shapes and labeling the corners of the shapes in the first column.

Cut out the three shapes at the bottom of the page. Using the shapes, create your own dot-transfer page.

Cut out the three shapes at the bottom of the page. Using the shapes, create your own dot-transfer page.

Cut out the three shapes at the bottom of the page. Using the shapes, create your own dot-transfer page.

Notes

Label and Transfer

Purpose: To label and visually transfer image.
Materials: Pencil and pages 66-69.
Vocabulary: Lines, spaces, label, congruent, transfer.

Activity: Label and Transfer Using a Grid, page 66

1. Discuss vocabulary — specifically what is meant by transfer of exact image.

2. Students transfer one box at a time to grid below.

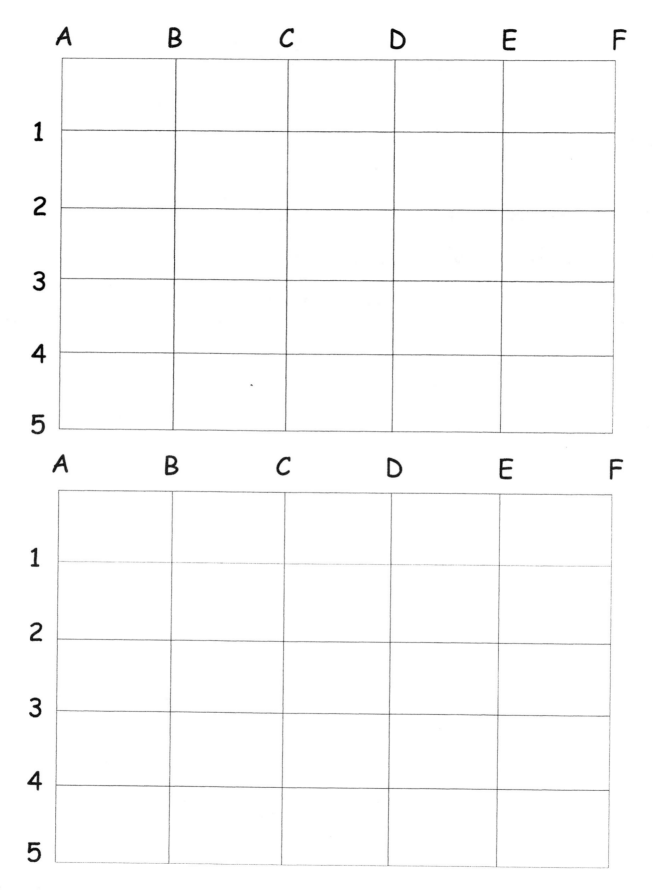

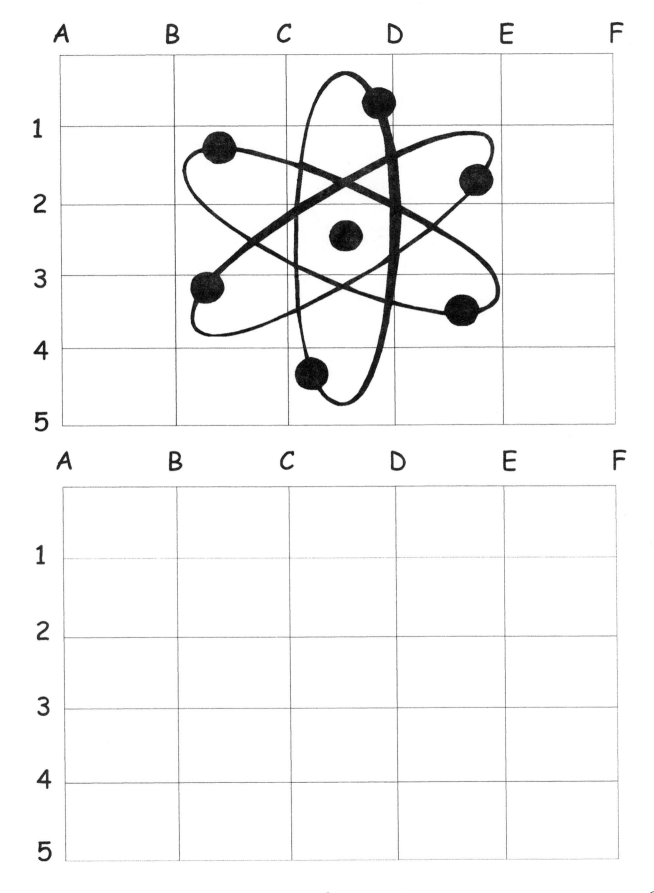

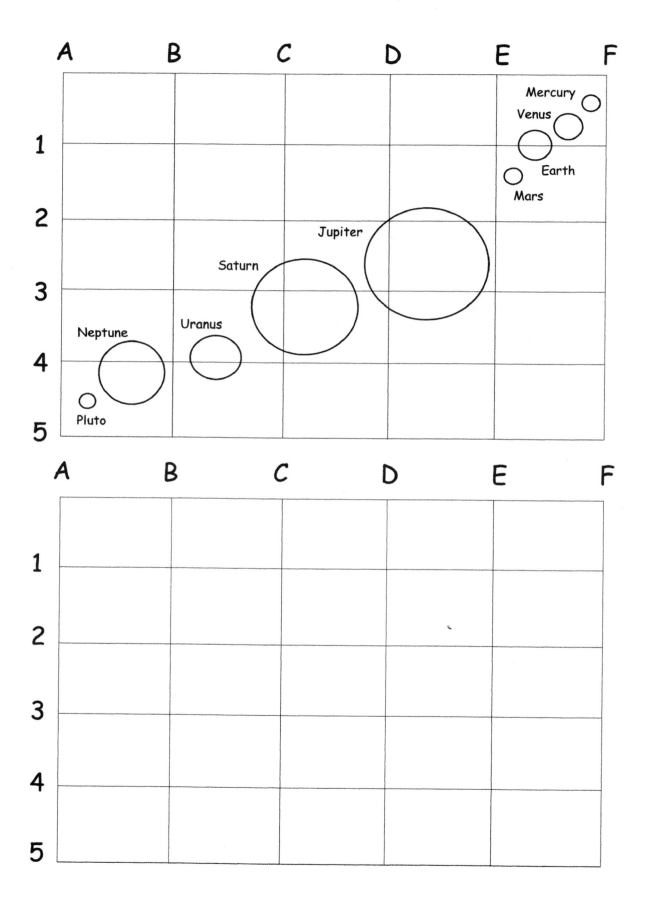

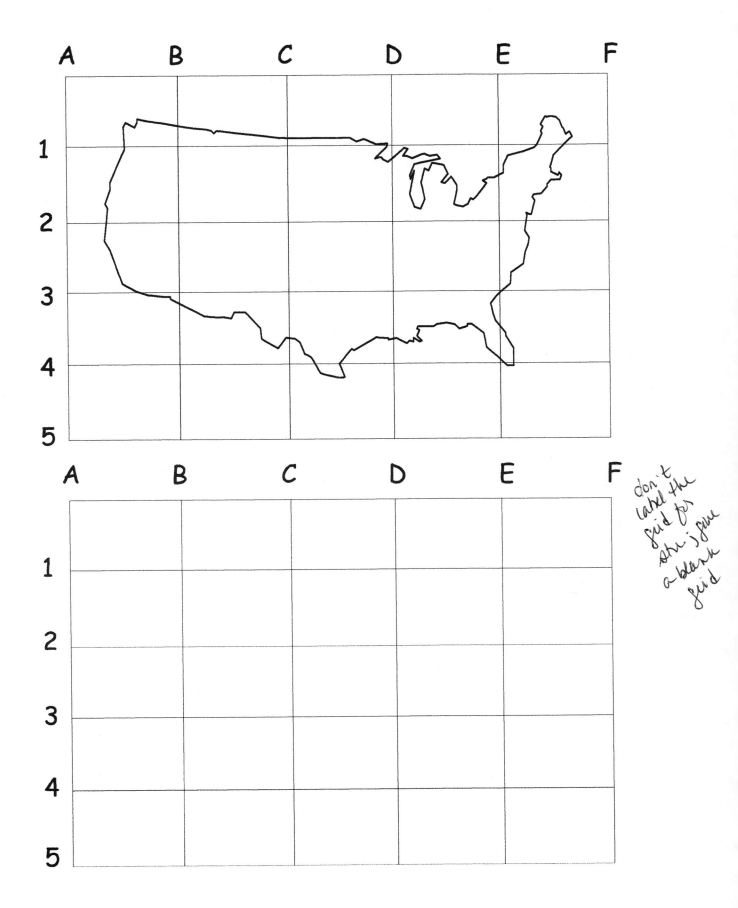

don't
label the
grid for
this game
a blank
grid

Payne lesson design

What

Vocabulary

Standard

Why

Connection to the Discipline (structure, purpose, pattern, process)

Mental Model (story, analogy, or drawing)

How

Instructional Plan/Activities
1.
2.
3.
4.
5.
6.

Steps student needs to take to do the tasks

Proof

_____ Question Making
_____ Rubrics
_____ Assessments
_____ Task completed

Mental Models
(Module 12)

Objective: To provide strategies for translating the abstract to the concrete.

Mental models can be:
- Two-dimensional visual representations.
- A story.
- A metaphor.

When mental models are directly taught for each discipline, abstract information can be learned much more quickly because the mind has a way to contain or hold the information.

Purpose: To demonstrate understanding of vocabulary words through sketching, thereby developing a mental model.

Materials: Paper, pencil, list of vocabulary words, dictionary.

Activity: Sketching Vocabulary, page 73 (primary example)

1. On the sheet provided, students will write the vocabulary words in the appropriate column.
2. Students will draw a brief sketch of the word.

Activity: Sketching Vocabulary, page 75 (intermediate example)

1. On the sheet provided, students will write the vocabulary words in the appropriate column.
2. Students will write in the next column what they think the word means.

3. Students will look up each word in the dictionary and write the definition in the space provided.
4. Students will draw sketches of the definition.
5. Students will use each word in a sentence.

Name: _____

Word	Picture

Name: _____

Word	Picture
log	
dog	
jog	
clog	
frog	
fog	
catalog	

Vocabulary

WORD	THINK?	MEANS	SKETCH

SENTENCE

Frayer Model
Visual Representations

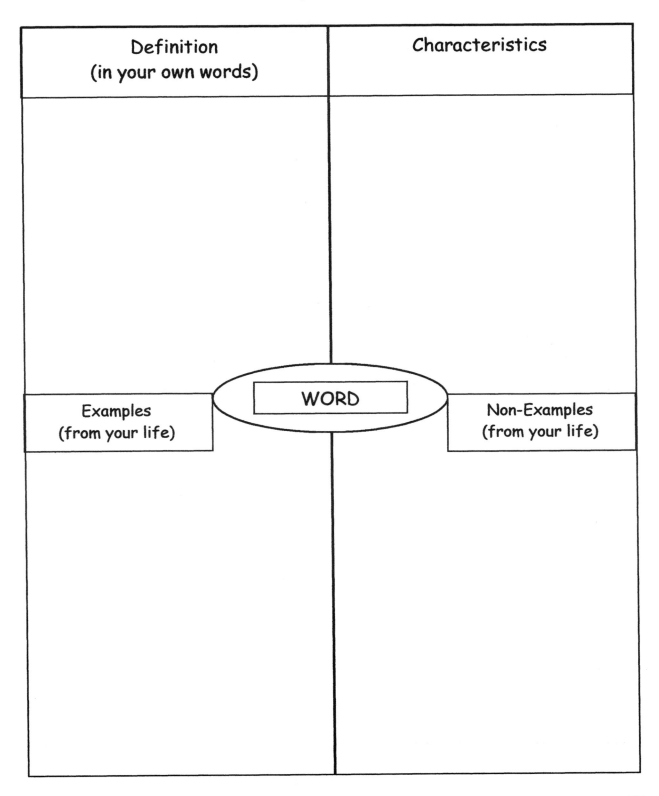

Definition (in your own words)	Characteristics

| Examples (from your life) | WORD | Non-Examples (from your life) |

Time

How do you see time?

8:00
8:30
9:00
9:30
10:00
10:30
11:00
11:30
12:00 Lunch
12:30
1:00
1:30
2:00
2:30
3:00

8:00 9:00 10:00 11:00 12:00 1:00 2:00 3:00

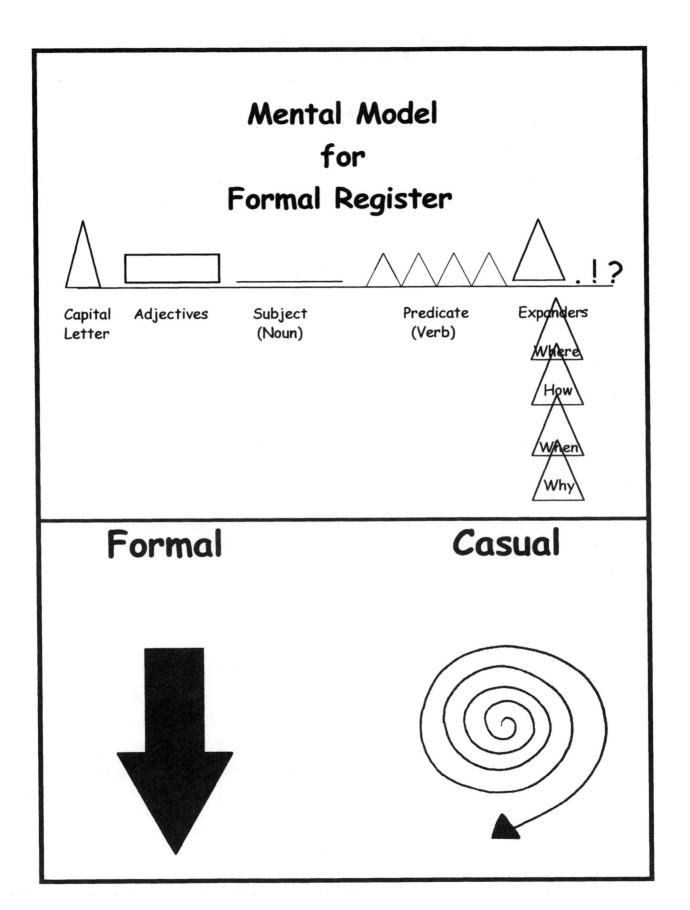

Mental Model
for
Formal Register

Capital Letter

Adjectives

Subject (Noun)

Predicate (Verb)

Expanders

Where

How

When

Why

Formal

Casual

Written Expression

Sentence Frame   /_____. ? !
       Reminds me that each sentence must contain a capital letter and some kind of punctuation mark.

Bare-Bones Sentence   /_____. ? !
       A sentence must contain a subject and an action.

The subject names a **person**, **place**, **thing**, or **idea**.

The action of the subject expresses **physical** or **mental** **action**:
     moved   kicked   thought   imagined

Predicate Expanders

The predicate can be expanded by expressing the

△ how   △ when   △ where   △ why of the action.

Example: The waves pounded relentlessly against the small sailboat because of the violent winds during the storm.

Where = prepositional phrases	to, from, against, behind
How = adverbs	-ly ending, like or as, with/without
When = time	before, during, after, when, while, since
Why = reason	because, to, so, for

(The opening sentence of each new paragraph should contain four expanders.)

Subject describers: Words that describe physical characteristics, personality, numbers, and ownership are describers.

Source: Contact Victoria Green or Mary Lee Enfield at Project Read: (800) 450-0343.

David's Father: Predicate Expander

WHERE

Purpose: To teach prepositional phrases as the expander *where.*
Materials: *David's Father* by Robert Munsch.

Application:

1. Read *David's Father* to students.

2. Help students build sentences, with the expander *where,* that
   relate to the story.
   Examples:
   Julie skipped.
   Julie skipped all the way home.
   They went into the kitchen.
   They stood in the middle of the sidewalk.
   They walked down the street.
   The cars jumped into the air.
   Father stomped down the sidewalk.

3. In worksheet form, students will complete the sentences, adding
   a *where* expander.
   1. Julie was skipping _____.
   2. She ran _____.
   3. Julie looked _____.
   4. Julie jumped _____.
   5. They went _____.
   6. They walked _____.
   7. The cars jumped _____.
   8. The big kids jumped _____.

4. Discuss the mobility of the expander *where.*
   Example: All the way home, Julie skipped.

Expanded Sentence

Use the model to create a sentence on the lines below.

_____

_____

_____

Change the location of one expander and rewrite the sentence.

_____

_____

_____

Gallon Guy

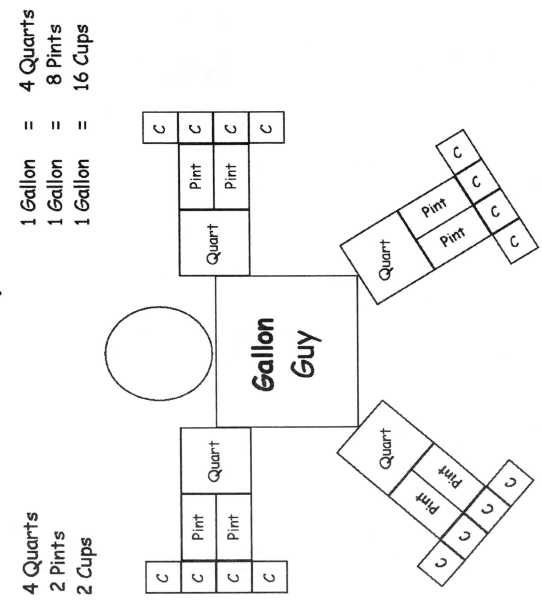

1 Gallon = 4 Quarts
1 Gallon = 8 Pints
1 Gallon = 16 Cups

1 Gallon = 4 Quarts
1 Quart = 2 Pints
1 Pint = 2 Cups

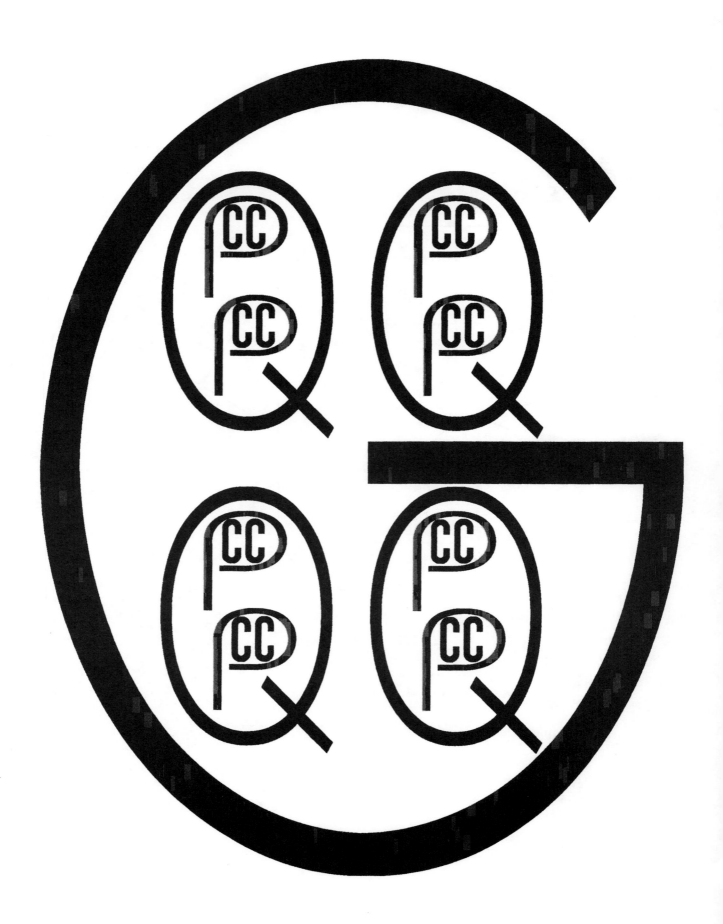

Mental Model for Rounding

The rounding rollercoaster is an easy way to teach the rounding of numbers. In rounding the number 783 to the nearest tens, we underline the 8 and circle the 3. The circled number is the one we locate on the rollercoaster.

7 8③
7 8 0

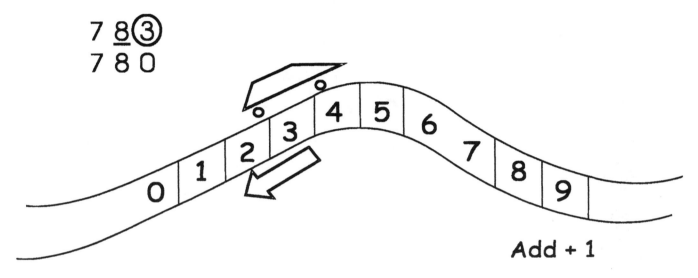

Add + 1

Stays the same

7⑧⑦
+1
8 0 0

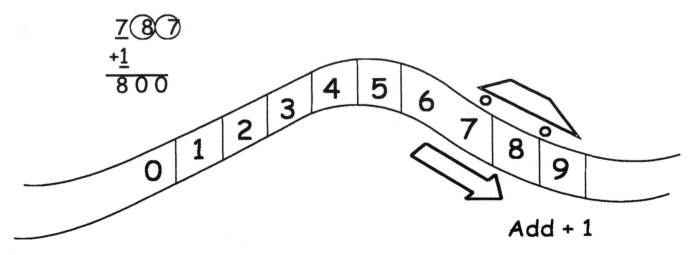

Add + 1

Stays the same

More Mental Models

Long division:

Dad	=	Divide	
Mom	=	Multiply	
Sister	=	Subtract	
Brother	=	Bring down	
Cousin	=	Check your work	
Rover	=	Repeat	

```
      3688
  2 | 7376
     -6
      13
     -12
      17
     -16
       16
      -16
        0
```

Model for Money
4 coins: quarter, dime, nickel, penny

● = 5 cents

4 coins with labels

Math Multiplication
+ and − numbers

In the first half of the equation:	In the second half of the equation:
+ numbers are good guys	+ numbers are coming to town
- numbers are bad guys	- numbers are leaving town

+ good guys	X	+ coming to town	= =	+ positive good
+ good guys	X	- leaving town	= =	- negative bad
- bad guys	X	+ coming to town	= =	- negative bad
- bad guys	X	- leaving town	= =	+ positive good

Math Multiplication
+ and − numbers

In the first half of the equation:	In the second half of the equation:
+ numbers are good guys	+ numbers are coming to town
− numbers are bad guys	− numbers are leaving town

+	X	+	=	+ positive
good guys		coming to town	=	good
8	x	8	=	64
+	X	−	=	− negative
good guys		leaving town	=	bad
8	x	−8	=	−64
−	X	+	=	− negative
bad guys		coming to town	=	bad
−8	x	8	=	−64
−	X	−	=	+ positive
bad guys		leaving town	=	good
−8	x	−8	=	+64

Planning to Control Impulsivity
(Module 13)

Objective: To teach students how to develop a plan.

If an individual depends upon a random, episodic story structure for memory patterns, lives in an unpredictable environment, and has not developed the ability to plan, then that individual may have trouble controlling impulsivity.

- If an individual cannot plan, he/she cannot predict.
- If an individual cannot predict, he/she cannot identify cause and effect.
- If an individual cannot identify cause and effect, he/she cannot identify consequence.
- If an individual cannot identify consequence, he/she cannot control impulsivity.
- If an individual cannot control impulsivity, he/she has an inclination toward criminal behavior.

–Adapted from Reuven Feuerstein

Activities on the following pages are examples of the following:
1. Plan, Do, Review ~~proof~~ → do this 2nd (plan for the day)
2. Picture - planning procedure for little kids
3. Step Sheets
4. Planning Backward → do this 1st (schedule your time)
5. Plan Your Grade — this step is for stu. w/out support @ home; so stu. take ownership = CONTRACT =
6. Rubric   goes w/#1
7. Self-Evaluation goes w/#1

Have stu. keep track of grades

1. Plan, [DO], Review ~ #6 rubric
                        #7 self-evaluation
                        PROOF

#3 step sheets

Name: _____
Daily plan: _____ Date: _____

1. My goal for the day is _____
_____

2. I will accomplish my goal by _____
_____

3. Today I did well on _____
_____

4. Tomorrow I need to practice _____
_____

5. I accomplished my goal. _____ Yes _____ No
6. My homework for tonight is _____
_____
_____

Name: _____
Daily plan: _____ Date: _____

1. My goal for the day is _____
_____

2. I will accomplish my goal by _____
_____

3. Today I did well on _____
_____

4. Tomorrow I need to practice _____
_____

5. I accomplished my goal. _____ Yes _____ No
6. My homework for tonight is _____
_____
_____

Name: _____

Weekly Plan: _____ Date: _____

1. My goal for the week is _____

_____.

2. To accomplish my goal I will:

    1. _____

    _____

    2. _____

    _____

    3. _____

    _____

    4. _____

    _____

3. This week I did well on _____

_____

_____.

4. Next week I need to work on _____

_____

_____.

5. I accomplished my goal. _____ Yes _____ No

Mental Model for Classificatory Writing

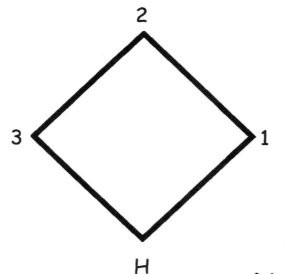

Team A
Advantages

Team B
Disadvantages

1. Opening sentence (H)
    Supporting sentence (1)
    Supporting sentence (2)
    Supporting sentence (3)
    Closing sentence (H)

2. Opening sentence
    Supporting sentence
    Supporting sentence
    Supporting sentence
    Closing sentence

3. Opening sentence
    Supporting sentence
    Supporting sentence
    Supporting sentence
    Closing sentence

1. Opening sentence (H)
    Supporting sentence (1)
    Supporting sentence (2)
    Supporting sentence (3)
    Closing sentence (H)

2. Opening sentence
    Supporting sentence
    Supporting sentence
    Supporting sentence
    Closing sentence

3. Opening sentence
    Supporting sentence
    Supporting sentence
    Supporting sentence
    Closing sentence

Research Calendar

March 1 Library	March 2 Library	March 3 Library	March 4 Library	March 5 Library
March 8	March 9	March 10 10 source cards due	March 11	March 12
March 15	March 16	March 17 Outline due	March 18	March 19
March 22	March 23	March 24	March 25	March 26
March 29	March 30	March 31 50 note cards due	April 1	April 2 Holiday
April 5 Holiday	April 6	April 7	April 8 Rough draft due	April 9
April 12	April 13	April 14	April 15	April 16
April 19	April 20	April 21	April 22 Final draft due	April 23 Oral presentation

Plan for Novel Unit

Test, visual, and oral presentation

Date: Oct 9
 	
Read to page 25
	Oct 10
	
	Read to page 40
		Oct 11
		
		Read to page 55
			Oct 12
			Mow grass —
			  help Dad
			Haircut
			Sat. night date
			  with Jenny

Oct 13
 	
Read to page 70
	Oct 14
	
	Read to page 85
		Oct 15
		Read to end of
		  book
		Work on
		  questions
			Oct 16
			Complete
			  questions
			Work on visual

Oct 17
 	
Make study guide
Review for test
	Oct 18
	Test
	Complete visual
	Outline for
	  presentation
		Oct 19
		Due:
		Visual and oral
		  presentation
			Oct 20

Checklist Completed	**Goal date**	**Date**
1. Book read.	10/15	_____
2. Questions answered.	10/16	_____
3. Study guide created.	10/17	_____
4. Visual for report finished.	10/18	_____
5. Outline for oral presentation written.	10/18	_____

Reading Contract

Setting goals will help me to be successful in all areas of life. To become a good reader, I must read daily.

My goal is to read _____ minutes each day. I will read carefully so that I can maintain an average of _____ on my independent reading tests and accumulate a total of _____ points by the end of each grading period.

	GOAL		ACTUAL	
	Grade	Points	Grade	Points
1st gr. period	_____	_____	_____	_____
2nd gr. period	_____	_____	_____	_____
3rd gr. period	_____	_____	_____	_____
4th gr. period	_____	_____	_____	_____

_____   _____
Student's name   Student's signature

_____   _____
Parent's signature   Teacher's signature

Informational Report

Thesis: _____

_____

Main point:

_____

_____

Supporting details/examples:
-
-
-

Main point:

_____

_____

Supporting details/examples:
-
-
-

Main point:

_____

_____

Supporting details/examples:
-
-
-

Conclusion:

_____

_____

_____

_____

What-to-Do-When-You-Get-Through List

1. Read, read, and read some more.

2. Write a story.

3. Write a letter to someone.

4. Write or copy a poem.

5. Write math story problems.

6. Write questions about your favorite story using the question-stems page.

7. Practice handwriting.

8. Work a puzzle.

9. Make a puzzle.

10. Transfer a puzzle on a grid.

11. Work a dots page.

12. Create a dots page.

13. Work a plan and label shapes page.

14. Create a plan and label shapes page.

15. Create a cartoon summary page.

16. Make a list of what you do best.

Notes

Plan and Label
for Academic Tasks
(Module 14)

Objective: To teach procedural plans for the content areas.

For a task to be done correctly, a student must have:
- A plan.
- A procedure.
- Labels (vocabulary).

Labels are the "tools" the mind uses to address the task.

Four ways to systematically label are:
- Numbering.
- Lettering.
- Assigning symbols.
- Color-coding.

The following activities can be used to help students plan and label.

Reading Strategies

1. Box in and read the title.
2. Trace and number the paragraphs.
3. Stop and think at the end of each paragraph to identify a key point.
4. Circle the key word or write the key point in the margin.
5. Read and label the key words in the questions. *what's it asking you?*
6. Prove your answer. Locate the paragraph where the answer is found.
7. Mark or write your answer.

1.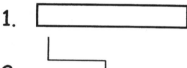

2.

3.   S   T

4.   ⬭

5.   👁 👁 and label

6.   P #

7.   ⬤

Baker Boy

When my father was a boy in northern Michigan, the annual Cherry Festival was an exciting event. The cherry pie baking contest always drew a large number of entries, including many from children. This allowed these beginning chefs a chance to practice for the future. The grand prize was a 6-inch-wide sweepstakes ribbon and the winner's picture featured on the front page of the county newspaper.

When my father was 11, he decided to enter the contest. No boy had ever won. In fact, no boy had ever entered! He was convinced he had the necessary cooking skills since he made his own breakfast every morning and had learned cooking measurements in school. Baking an award-winning pie didn't sound difficult to him at all.

For weeks he saved his money to buy the things that would be needed. He read recipe books and talked to friends of his grandmother to find out their secrets. Mrs. Johannsen told him how he must handle the crust like a delicate china dish. Mrs. Bowen confided that her secret ingredient was almond flavoring in the filling to give it a special taste. He thought about all these tips as he planned his project.

By the day before the contest, he had practiced rolling out piecrust eight times. He never doubted that he could win.

The day of the contest, he got up before the sun rose. All morning he mixed flour, sugar, shortening, spices, cherries, creamery butter from their farm, and the secret weapon, almond flavoring. He made two pies, in order to have double the chance of getting a perfect one for the contest.

The pies baked in the oven for 45 minutes. Finally the timer rang, and he opened the door. There were two of the most perfect golden-crusted pies that he had ever seen.

When my father presented his best pie to the committee, there was quite a stir. After lunch the judges closed the doors to the hall and began their deliberation. They had to taste each pie and judge it on its flaky crust, tasty filling, and mouth-watering spices. Two hours later they announced their decision. No. 5 had won! Imagine everyone's surprise when the judges presented the blue ribbon to an 11-year-old boy!

Texas Assessment of Academic Skills, 1996

Baker Boy

1 When my father was a boy in northern Michigan, the annual Cherry Festival was an exciting event. The cherry pie baking contest always drew a large number of entries, including many from children. This allowed these beginning chefs a chance to practice for the future. The grand prize was a 6-inch-wide sweepstakes ribbon and the winner's picture featured on the front page of the county newspaper.

2 When my father was 11, he decided to enter the contest. No boy had ever won. In fact, no boy had ever entered! He was convinced he had the necessary cooking skills since he made his own breakfast every morning and had learned cooking measurements in school. Baking an award-winning pie didn't sound difficult to him at all.

3 For weeks he saved his money to buy the things that would be needed. He read recipe books and talked to friends of his grandmother to find out their secrets. Mrs. Johannsen told him how he must handle the crust like a delicate china dish. Mrs. Bowen confided that her secret ingredient was almond flavoring in the filing to give it a special taste. He thought about all these tips as he planned his project.

4 By the day before the contest, he had practiced rolling out pie crust eight times. He never doubted that he could win.

5 The day of the contest, he got up before the sun rose. All morning he mixed flour, sugar, shortening, spices, cherries, creamery butter from their farm, and the secret weapon, almond flavoring. He made two pies, in order to have double the chance of getting a perfect one for the contest.

6 The pies baked in the oven for 45 minutes. Finally the timer rang, and he opened the door. There were two of the most perfect golden-crusted pies that he had ever seen.

7 When my father presented his best pie to the committee, there was quite a stir. After lunch the judges closed the doors to the hall and began their deliberation. They had to taste each pie and judge it on its flaky crust, tasty filling, and mouth-watering spices. Two hours later they announced their decision. No. 5 had won! Imagine everyone's surprise when the judges presented the blue ribbon to an 11-year-old boy!

Texas Assessment of Academic Skills 1996

Self-Questioning Strategies

Place the following symbols in the text where you find the answers:

☺ = Who

⇨ = Where

☐ = What

Y = Why

☀ = When

H = How

Write one sentence for each symbol below.

☺ _____

_____

⇨ _____

_____

☀ _____

_____

Y _____

_____

☐ _____

_____

H _____

_____

Title:

Author:

Setting:	Three main characters:	Conflict or problem:
Time Place		
Events Beginning	Middle	End

www.ahaprocess.com

Story Map

Draw and label three characters in the book:

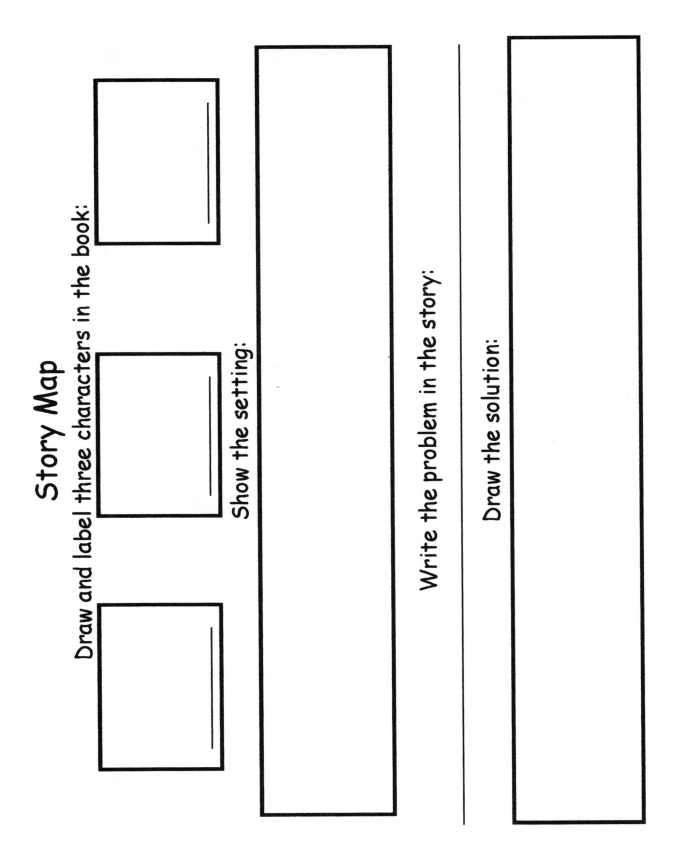

Show the setting:

Write the problem in the story:

Draw the solution:

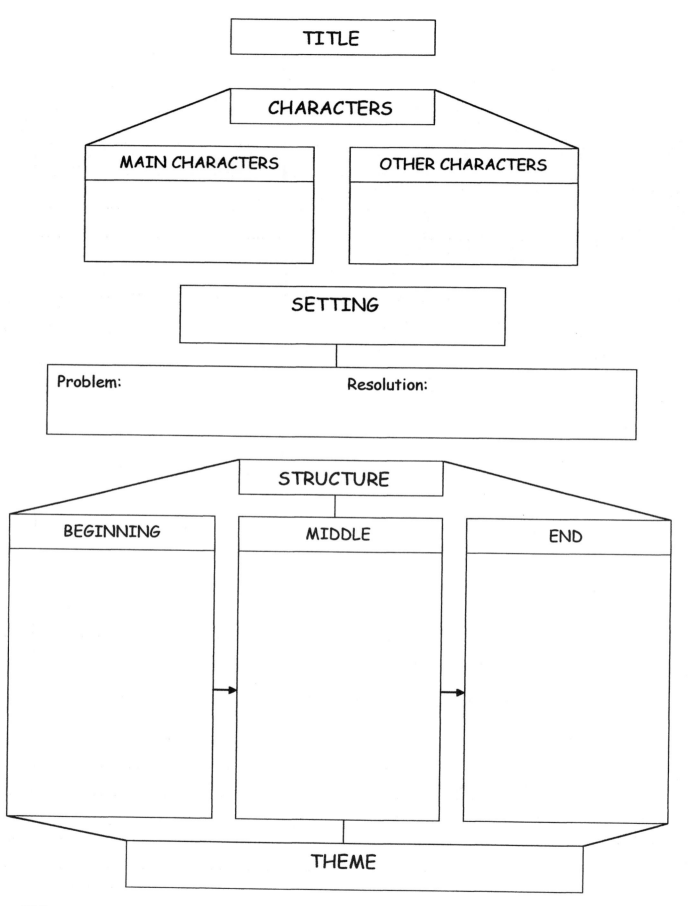

TITLE

CHARACTERS

MAIN CHARACTERS

OTHER CHARACTERS

SETTING

Problem: Resolution:

STRUCTURE

BEGINNING   MIDDLE   END

THEME

Story Plot Chart

Title:
Author:
Setting:
    Time:
    Place:
    General:
    Specific:

Problem or goal:

Circle one:

MAN against MAN   MAN against NATURE   MAN against SELF

Events:
1.
2.
3.
4.
5.

Event that solved the problem:

Message of theme:

Narrative Writing

	Yes	Not yet
Setting /When\ & /Where\		
Characters described		
Problem/conflict		
Events 1, 2, 3, 4, 5		
Solution/conclusion		
Strong, vivid language Subject describers		
Fluency (_____ words)		
Legibility		

www.ahaprocess.com

Classificatory Writing

	Yes	Not yet
Opening (restate prompt)		
Three good things/advantages (two sentences per idea)		
Three bad things/disadvantages (two sentences per idea)		
△ Why **Six "why" statements**		
Conclusion (restate prompt)		
Vivid language (10 examples) Subject describers Adjectives		
Legibility		
Fluency # of words counted _____ # required _____		

Writing Rubric Based on Indiana Writing Standards and Rubric

	Ideas & Content	Organization	Voice	Style	Language in Use
4	* stays focused on topic * includes complete relevant ideas and information	* has very clear order	* effectively adjusts language and tone to task and reader	* exhibits exceptional word usage * is very fluent and easy to read * displays strong sense of reader appeal	* few or no capitalization errors * subject/verb agreement * few or no run-on sentences/fragments * few or no punctuation errors * few or no paragraphing errors * few or no spelling errors * uses time order/transition words correctly
3	* stays mostly focused on topic * includes some relevant information	* has order	* attempts to adjust language and tone to task and reader	* exhibits adequate word usage * is fluent * displays some sense of reader appeal	* most capitalization is correct * most subjects/verbs agree * may have run-on sentences/fragments * most punctuation is correct * most paragraphing is correct * most spelling is correct * uses some time order/transition words
2	* stays somewhat focused on topic * includes few relevant ideas and information	* has some order	* attempts somewhat to adjust language and tone to task and reader	* exhibits minimal word usage * is somewhat fluent * displays little sense of reader appeal	* some capitalization is correct * some subjects/verbs agree * several run-on sentences/fragments * some punctuation is correct * some paragraphing is correct * some spelling is correct * uses few time order/transition words
1	* has little or no focus on topic * includes almost no relevant ideas and information	* has little or no order	* may use language and tone inappropriate to task and reader	* exhibits less than minimal word usage * is hard to read * displays little or no sense of reader appeal	* many capitalization errors * little or no subject/verb agreement * many run-on sentences/fragments * many punctuation errors/missing/incorrect * paragraphs missing * many spelling errors * uses no time order/transition words

Kindergarten Writing Rubric

Name _____	All of the time	Almost always	Usually	Occasionally	Rarely/ never
	5	4	3	2	1
• Writes on the page from left to right.					
• Writes on the page from top to bottom.					
• Talks about writing.					
• Uses spaces between words.					
• Matches picture to text.					
• Expresses a complete thought.					
• Chooses a topic.					
• Prints lower-case letters.					
• Prints capital letters.					
• Copies words correctly from other sources.					
• Attempts to have beginning and ending sounds in words.					
• Writes words using beginning sounds.					
TOTAL					
AVERAGE (Sum of the total divided by 13)					

Comments: _____

_____

_____

Writing Evaluation

Name _____

Assignment _____

Date _____

	4	3	2	1
	Excellent	Good	Fair	Poor
Follows assignment				
Clear beginning, middle, and end				
Creative/details				
Descriptive word choice				
Sequence/organization				
Variety of sentences				
Complete sentences				
Proper punctuation/capitalization				
Grammar/spelling				
Neatness				
Total column points				

Total of all columns: _____   Grade: _____

A+ = 40 points   B+ = 32-34   C+ = 22-24   D+ = 13-14
A = 37-39   B = 28-31   C = 18-21   D = 11-12
A- = 35-36   B- = 25-27   C- = 15-17   D- = 10

Comments:

Student: _____

English Paper
Major Grade
DUE FRIDAY, AUGUST 23, 2004

Objective: To select a significant moment in your life and write a narrative paper about that moment.

Procedure:
1. Make a timeline of significant events in your life.
2. Select one.
3. Write a rough draft.
4. Share the rough draft with two others.
5. Revise.
6. Write your final copy.
7. Put in the following order to turn in: Final copy
   Timeline
   Revised copy
   Student response sheet

Criteria:

1. Neat appearance		yes	no
2. Catchy title		yes	no
3. Shows beginning, middle, and end of event		yes	no
4. Narration keeps attention of reader		yes	no
5. Uses dialog		yes	no
6. Spelling is correct		yes	no
7. Eliminates fragments/run-ons		yes	no
8. Revisions are evident		yes	no
9. All parts included		yes	no
10. Long enough		yes	no

Penalties:
-10, Monday, Aug. 26
-20, Tuesday, Aug. 27
50 max score, Aug. 28 - Sept. 24

Bonus: + 5 if word-processed

Research Review

1. My reading journal shows that I read ____ books to learn about my topic. The most helpful books were:

_____

_____

2. My research cards show that I learned about the following topics:

    1. _____ *

    2. _____ *

    3. _____ *

    4. _____ *

    5. _____

        * required

3. My illustration shows:

_____

_____

_____

4. Based on the rubric, I would rate my project a ____ because: _____

_____

_____

5. My favorite part of the project is _____

_____

Term Paper Planning

Topic: _____

Length: _____

Numbers of sources:

    Primary _____

    Secondary _____

Steps →	→	→	→	→
Estimated time				
Target date	←	←	←	←
Date assigned				Deadline

Use an atlas, almanac, encyclopedia, or other source to complete the chart about your state.

State name:	Draw your state flag in the box below.
State nickname:	
Capital:	
Largest city:	
Populations of: State _____ Largest city _____	
Land area:	

In the boxes below, draw the following symbols:

State flower	State tree	State bird

Draw a picture of what you might see if you were on vacation in this state.

Poster Evaluation
State Report

STATE: _____

State/title	2 points	_____
State capital	1 point	_____
State bird	1 point	_____
State flower	1 point	_____
State tree	1 point	_____
State song	1 point	_____
State logo	1 point	_____
State nickname	1 point	_____
Draw and color flag	3 points	_____
Draw and color flower	2 points	_____

Three products of state

_____	1 point	_____
_____	1 point	_____
_____	1 point	_____
Neatness	2 points	_____
Fill space on poster	1 point	_____

Bonus:

Extra drawings	1 point	_____
Extra information	1 point	_____
_____	1 point	_____
	TOTAL	_____
	GRADE	_____

21 +	A +	17	B+	14	C+	11	D+	
19-20	A	16	B	13	C	10	D	
18	A-	15	B-	12	C-	Below	10	F

Response Sheet

As you listen, write down interesting information about each state.

1. Student: _____
   State: _____
   Capital: _____
   Information: _____
   _____

2. Student: _____
   State: _____
   Capital: _____
   Information: _____
   _____

3. Student: _____
   State: _____
   Capital: _____
   Information: _____
   _____

4. Student: _____
   State: _____
   Capital: _____
   Information: _____
   _____

Math

Think ???

What function is needed?

Which words give me clues?

Read the **question** carefully.

Information

Circle the numbers I will need.

Mark out irrelevant text.

Plan

What is my plan?

What model will I use?

How will I show my work?

Solution

Recheck all information before writing answer.

Problem-Solving Process

Step 1: READ THE PROBLEM
- Read the problem through completely to determine what it's asking.

Step 2: REREAD THE PROBLEM AND QUESTION
- Reread to visualize the problem.
- Highlight or mark the question with a wavy line.

Step 3: MARK YOUR INFORMATION
- Box the action or important words.
- Circle needed information.
- Loop out extra information.

Step 4: CHOOSE AN APPROPRIATE STRATEGY FOR THE PROBLEM
- Choose an operation.
- Solve a simpler problem.
- Make an organized list.
- Look for a pattern.
- Guess and check.
- Use logical reasoning.
- Make a table.
- Use objects.
- Draw a picture.
- Act it out.
- Work backward.

Step 5: SOLVE
- Solve the problem.

Step 6: IS THE QUESTION ANSWERED?
- Read the question again.
- Does the solution answer the question?
- Does it make sense?
- Is it reasonable?
- Check by using a different strategy if possible.

Source: Judy Sain, *Daily Math Practice*

Problem-Solving Worksheet

What is the question?
List what you know (data, numbers).
What is your plan?
Show your work.
Solution.

Problem-Solving Rubric

RATING	6	5	4	3	2	1
TASK	Completed the task	Completed most of the task	Completed some of the task	Completed very little of the task	Did not understand the task	No attempt
PLAN	Used one or more helpful strategy	Used at least one helpful strategy	Used a helpful strategy but did not use the strategy correctly	Used a strategy that was not helpful	Did not use a strategy	No attempt
WORK	All work included and labeled clearly	Most work included and most work labeled clearly	Some work included and some work labeled	Very little work included and very little work labeled	No work included	No attempt
COMPUTATION	No mistakes	One mistake	Two mistakes	Three mistakes	More than three mistakes	No attempt
COMMUNICATION	Clear and effective explanation with detailed steps Accurate use of mathematical representation, terminology, and notation	Clear explanation Some use of mathematical representation, terminology, and notation	Incomplete explanation Some use of mathematical representation, terminology, and notation	Incomplete explanation — may not be clearly represented Little use of mathematical representation, terminology, and notation	No explanation or not represented correctly No use of mathematical representation, terminology, or notation	No attempt

Science Four-Question Strategy

Materials	Action
Change	Measure

1. What materials are available?

2. How do these materials act or what will they do (melt, grow, bounce, etc.)?

3. How can you change the materials so that they will act differently?

4. How will you measure the changes?

Source: Marie Smith

Name: _____   Date: _____

Basic Concepts of Design
100 points

Criteria	Value	Self	Peer	Teacher
Title	5			
Hypothesis	5			
Independent variable	10			
Levels of independent variable	10			
Control	10			
Repeated trials	10			
Dependent variable	10			
Operational definitions of dependent variables	10			
Constants	15			
Experimental design diagram	10			
Creativity/complexity	5			
Totals	100	____	____	____

Source: Marie Smith

www.ahaprocess.com

Response Sheet

Name of author: _____

Title of paper: _____

Name of responder: _____

My three favorite parts: Three specific suggestions for improvement:

☺   1.

☺   2.

☺   3.

Name of responder: _____

My three favorite parts: Three specific suggestions for improvement:

☺   1.

☺   2.

☺   3.

Television Response Journal

While watching television, determine a program's intent, target audience, and type. Explain whether the show succeeds or fails in its purpose.

---

1. Program title:

Intent (circle one):

informs   entertains   persuades   interprets events   transmits culture

Target audience: age _____   specific group _____

This program attempts to _____

by_____

_____

Was the program successful? Why or why not? _____

_____

---

2. Program title:

Intent (circle one) :

informs   entertains   persuades   interprets events   transmits culture

Target audience: age _____   specific group _____

This program attempts to _____

by _____

_____

Was the program successful? Why or why not? _____

_____

---

3. Program title:

Intent (circle one):

informs   entertains   persuades   interprets events   transmits culture

Target audience: age _____   specific group

_____

This program attempts to _____

by _____

Was the program successful? Why or why not? _____

_____

Reflection

NAME: _____ DATE: _____

TOPIC: _____

Source of Information:

☐ Text ☐ Discussion ☐ Speech ☐ Lecture

☐ Video ☐ Graphic ☐ Internet ☐ Other _____

1. Key points:

- _____
- _____
- _____
- _____

2. One insight, thought, or reflection:

_____

_____

3. How this applies to my life:

_____

_____

4. How this relates to other subjects:

_____

_____

5. Questions concerning the information:

- _____
- _____
- _____

Applying Bloom's Taxonomy of Cognitive Process
Activities and Products

KNOWLEDGE
- List the story's main events.
- Make a timeline of events.
- Make a facts chart.
- List any pieces of information you remember.
- Recite a poem.
- List all the animals in the story.
- Make a chart showing . . .
- Make an acrostic.

COMPREHENSION
- Cut out or draw pictures to show a particular event.
- Illustrate the main idea.
- Make a cartoon strip showing the sequence of events.
- Write and perform a play based on the story.
- Make a coloring book.
- Retell the story in your own words.
- Paint a picture of some aspect of the story you like.
- Write a summary of the event.
- Prepare a flow chart to illustrate the sequence of events.

APPLICATION
- Construct a model to demonstrate how it will work.
- Make a diorama to illustrate an important event.
- Compose a book about . . .
- Make a scrapbook about the areas of study.
- Make a papier-mâché map showing information about an event.
- Make a puzzle game using ideas from the study area.
- Make a clay model or paint a mural.
- Design a marketing strategy for your product.

ANALYSIS

- Design a questionnaire to gather information.
- Make a flow chart to show critical stages.
- Write a commercial for a new or familiar product.
- Review a work of art in terms of form, color, and texture.
- Construct a graph to illustrate selected information.
- Construct a jigsaw puzzle.
- Analyze a family tree showing relationships.
- Write a biography about a person being studied.
- Arrange a party and record/list the steps you took.

SYNTHESIS

- Invent a machine to do a specific task.
- Design a building.
- Create a new product. Give it a name and marketing plan.
- Write about your feelings in relation to . . .
- Write a TV show, play, puppet show, song, or pantomime about . . .
- Design a record, book, or magazine cover.
- Devise a way to . . .
- Create a language code.
- Compose a rhythm or put new words to a known melody.

EVALUATION

- Prepare a list of criteria to judge a show.
- Conduct a debate about an area of special interest.
- Make a booklet about five rules you value.
- Form a panel to discuss a topic. State criteria.
- Write a letter to _____ advising changes needed.
- Prepare arguments to present your view about . . .

Notes

Question Making
(Module 15)

Objective: To teach students the process of writing and understanding questions.

- To perform any task, one must be able to go inside the head to formulate and ask questions.

- If individuals cannot ask questions, then they cannot examine any behavior, nor can they retrieve information in a systematic way.

Students must be able to formulate questions syntactically; without this ability, the mind literally cannot know what it knows.

The following activities can be used to help students learn the skill of formulating questions.

Rules for Question Making

Question:

_____

_____

Answers:

A. _____

B. _____

C. _____

D. _____

Question:

_____

_____

Answers:

A. _____

B. _____

C. _____

D. _____

Rules:

1. Only one right answer.
2. One wrong answer may be funny.
3. May *not* use "all of the above" or "none of the above."

Question Making

With a partner, roll the die to determine the type of question to write.

1. Who?
2. Where?
3. What?
4. When?
5. How?
6. Your choice.

Question: _____

_____

A. _____
B. _____
C. _____
D. _____

Question: _____

_____

A. _____
B. _____
C. _____
D. _____

Whales

Did you know that some whales do not have teeth? The baleen whales do not have teeth but have hundreds of thin plates in their mouth instead. These plates, called baleen, strain out food from the water.

Baleen whales eat plankton — tiny animal and plant life that drifts in the ocean. The blue whale, the largest animal in the world today, is a baleen whale. It may grow to be 100 feet in length.

Many other whales have teeth and are called toothed whales. They eat squid, fish, and other creatures. Toothed whales use their teeth to catch their prey, but they swallow their food whole instead of chewing it. The male narwhal is perhaps the strangest-looking of the toothed whales. It has one tooth that grows out of its upper lip, forming a long, twisted tusk.

Write a multiple-choice question, along with three wrong answers, for the correct answer below.

1. Q _____
   a. _____
   b. Baleen whales eat tiny plant and animal life called plankton.
   c. _____
   d. _____

2. Q _____
   a. _____
   b. _____
   c. The blue whale may grow as long as 100 feet.
   d. _____

3. Q _____
   a. Toothed whales swallow their food whole instead of chewing.
   b. _____
   c. _____
   d. _____

How Do Plants Trap and Eat Insects?

A plant that eats insects? Can it be true? Yes, it can! There are some plants that trap and digest insects in order to live. These carnivorous plants feed on animal life.

All plants need a chemical called nitrate in order to grow. Most can get nitrate right from the ground, but soils in such damp places as swamps do not have much nitrate, so some plants that live in swamps get nitrate by eating insects.

Venus Flytrap

One plant that eats insects is the Venus flytrap. On the edges of its leaves are sharp thorns that look like claws. Each leaf has little hairs on it. When the hairs are touched, the leaf folds itself in half. The claws lock together and the insect cannot get out. A special liquid inside the plant helps digest the insect.

Sundew Plant

The sundew plant also has leaves that are covered with little hairs. On each of these hairs is a drop of very sticky liquid. When the sun shines on the plant, the liquid sparkles and attracts insects, but any insect that touches the plant is stuck for sure! The sundew plant's hairs close slowly and a special liquid digests the insect.

Pitcher Plant

The pitcher plant does not just trap insects, it drowns them! This plant is shaped like a tube and catches rainwater. Insects are attracted to it because of a sweet, honey-like liquid. The liquid is slippery and insects have to work hard not to slide in. After a while they become tired, fall down the tube, and drown.

These strange plants show that there are many ways for plants to get food to live and grow.

Using the information about insect-eating plants, write one correct and three incorrect answers to the following questions.

1. What happens when an insect lands on the leaf of a Venus flytrap?
    A. _____
    B. _____
    C. _____
    D. _____

2. The word "carnivorous" in this passage means
    A. _____
    B. _____
    C. _____
    D. _____

3. The plants in this passage feed on insects because the insects
    A. _____
    B. _____
    C. _____
    D. _____

4. You are most likely to find the insect-eating plants in
    A. _____
    B. _____
    C. _____
    D. _____

5. Which of these is a FACT about insect-eating plants?
    A. _____
    B. _____
    C. _____
    D. _____

www.ahaprocess.com

Reading-Question Stems

Word meaning:
    In this story, the word _____ means . . . ?
    The word _____ in this passage means . . . ?

Supporting ideas:
    What did _____ do after . . . ?
    What happened just before _____ . . . ?
    What did _____ do first?
    Where does this story take place?
    When does the story take place?

Summarizing written texts:
    Which sentence tells the main idea of the story?
    This story is mainly about . . . ?
    What is the main idea of paragraph ____ ?
    Which statement best summarizes this passage (paragraph)?

Perceiving relationships and recognizing outcomes:
    Why did _____ (name) do _____ (action)?
    What will happen as a result of _____ ?
    Based on the information, which is _____ most likely to do?
    What will happen to _____ in this story?
    You can tell from this passage that _____ is most likely to . . . ?

Analyzing information to make inferences and generalizations:
    How did _____ feel about _____ ?
    How does _____ feel at the beginning (end) of the story?
    According to Figure 1, what . . . ? (where, when, how many?)
    By _____ (action), _____ (name) was able to show that . . . ?
    The _____ (event) is being held in order to . . . ?
    You can tell from this passage that . . . ?
    Which word best describes _____ feelings in this passage?
    Which of these is a fact expressed in this passage?
    Which of these is an opinion expressed in this passage?

Divergent Questioning Model Stems

Quantity model:
> How many ways ...?
> List the reasons for ...
> List all of the ...

Viewpoint model:
> How would this look to a ...?
> What would this look like to a ...?
> What would _____ think about _____?

Involvement model:
> How would you feel if you were _____?
> You are a _____. What does _____ feel like from your point of view?
> How would it feel if it were human?

Forced association model:
> How is _____ like a _____?
> How can you get ideas from _____ to help you work on _____?
> How would _____ be like a _____ if _____ changed?

Reorganization model:
> What would happen if _____?
> Suppose _____ occurred. What would be the consequences?

- Remember that the quantity model is simply brainstorming.
- Write out questions in advance.
- Do not try to use more than one type of question per lesson.
- Require "Just a moment, let me think" before the students respond.

Source: Marie Smith

Bloom's Taxonomy

Knowledge	"I know." List, recite, tell, name, label, record, copy, report, memorize, define, select, why, when, where, who
Comprehension	"I understand." Describe, translate, summarize, infer, interpret, locate, identify, recognize, review, describe, restate, explain, report, define, indicate, translate, match
Application	"I can use the information." Do, act out, dramatize, personalize, solve, apply, illustrate, translate, interview, operate, practice, demonstrate how, identify, construct
Analysis	"I can break down the information." Analyze, dissect, compare, contrast, experiment, diagram, categorize, differentiate, criticize, debate, solve, inventory, arrange, conclude, distinguish, investigate, what is related/not related, what is similar
Synthesis	"I can create." Create, design, invent, compose, prepare, predict, formulate, hypothesize, plan, organize, elaborate, estimate, dance, build, forecast, blend, infer, imagine, combine, construct, solve, what if?
Evaluation	"I can make judgments based on information given." Evaluate, choose, criticize, select, estimate, appraise, value, predict, editorialize, judge, rate, defend, grade, dispute, verify, decide

U R TOPS
Strategy for Open-Response Questions

HAPPEN BEFORE WRITING

U	**UNDERLINE**	UNDERLINE or highlight key words, ideas, power verbs, and important information.
R	**READ**	READ everything twice before you start to answer. Read charts, diagrams, and maps, then reread the question.
T	**TOPIC SENTENCE**	Create a TOPIC SENTENCE that clearly states your position, decision, or starts your answer.
O	**ORGANIZE**	ORGANIZE your thoughts to answer the question. Be clear, concise, and to the point.
P	**PART**	Look for specific PARTS to be answered. Label each part with a number.
S	**SUPPORT**	SUPPORT your answer with facts, figures, or statements from what is given. Show all problem-solving steps.

Social Studies Open-Response Questions

Write your answer on a separate sheet of paper. Use the cartoon below to answer the question.

The United States is often called "a nation of immigrants." Today many people still seek to emigrate to the United States.

A. Describe the cartoonist's point of view about emigration to the U.S. Be sure to mention the symbols that show his view.

B. Discuss two reasons why people might want to leave their homeland and two reasons why they might want to come to the U.S.

Sample state assessment question

Question Making
for Math

Use the following information to create a problem-solving question.

A pet store has two tanks of goldfish and five tanks of tropical fish. There are 15 fish in each tank. The fish eat every morning and night.

Question: _____

_____

A. _____

B. _____

C. _____

D. _____

Use the same information to create a different problem.

Question: _____

_____

A. _____

B. _____

C. _____

D. _____

www.ahaprocess.com

Robert E. Lee Choir

Use the information from the chart to create two problem-solving questions.

Question: _____

_____

A. _____

B. _____

C. _____

D. _____

Question: _____

_____

A. _____

B. _____

C. _____

D. _____

Math Distractors

Math distractors are:

- Incorrect operation

- Incorrect order

- Decimal in wrong place

- Answer in wrong form (percent instead of number, etc.)

- Missed step

- Unnecessary information included

- Computational errors

Sorting Strategies
(Module 16)

Objective: To teach students how to sort concrete and abstract information.

To sort and retrieve information, one must be able to sort using criteria and patterns.

Criteria may be based on:

Structure	Purpose
Number	Size
Direction	Color
Shape	Detail
Type	Pattern
Function	Design

The following activities can be used ... did you want to say anything more about sorting?

On a separate sheet of paper, list three ways in which the pictures in each row are alike and three ways they are different.

1.

2.

3.

4.

www.ahaprocess.com

1   Alike   Different

    1. _____   _____
    2. _____   _____
    3. _____   _____

2   Alike   Different

    1. _____   _____
    2. _____   _____
    3. _____   _____

3   Alike   Different

    1. _____   _____
    2. _____   _____
    3. _____   _____

4   Alike   Different

    1. _____   _____
    2. _____   _____
    3. _____   _____

Degrees of Meaning

Choose four vocabulary words. Look up each word in a thesaurus. Find five synonyms or related words for your original word. Make a chart of the degrees of meaning by filling in the words on the thermometer.

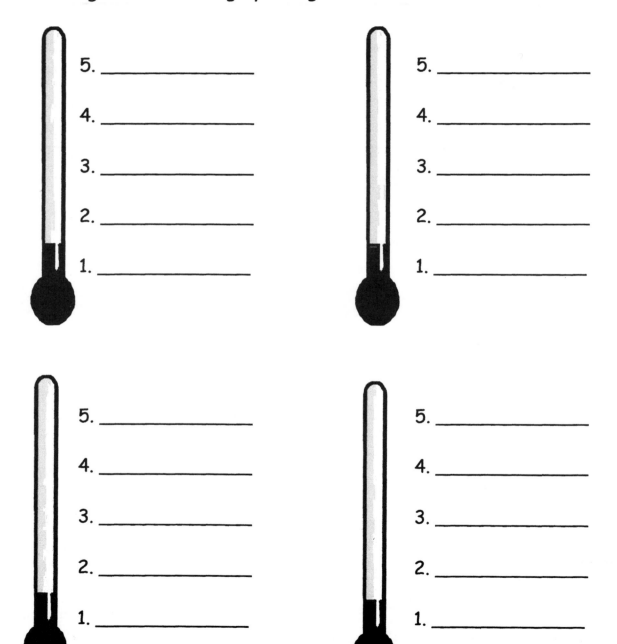

5. _____

4. _____

3. _____

2. _____

1. _____

5. _____

4. _____

3. _____

2. _____

1. _____

5. _____

4. _____

3. _____

2. _____

1. _____

5. _____

4. _____

3. _____

2. _____

1. _____

Character Contrast Chart

Character		
Appearance		
Education		
Family		
Religion		
Fears		
Actions		

Sorting Words

Fill in the chart below using general or specific words as indicated by the blank spaces.

General	Specific
Animal	
	1967 Ford Mustang
Fun	
Thing	
	Terrified
Lazy	
Fast	
	Sizzling hot
	Ecstatic

Choose three words for your own chart. Trade with your partner and complete each other's chart.

General	Specific

Source: Connie Abernathy

Sorting Words

Fill in the chart below using general or specific words as indicated by the blank spaces.

General	Specific

Choose three words for your own chart. Trade with your partner and Complete each other's chart.

General	Specific

Sorting Model for Author's Purpose

What was the author's purpose for writing this book? Gather information and evidence under each category to help you decide which purpose best suits this book.

To inform	
To teach	
To entertain	
To elicit an emotional response	

Tell what you think the author's purpose was for writing this book. Use examples from the story to explain your thinking. _____

_____

_____

_____

_____

www.ahaprocess.com

Five Models to Use
for Sorting

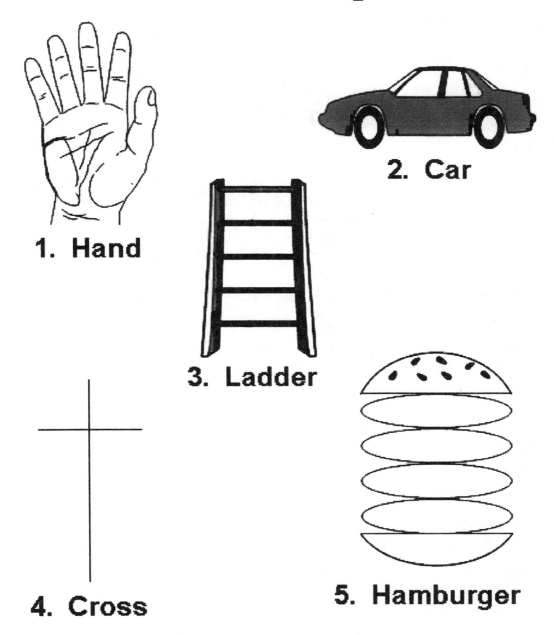

1. Hand

2. Car

3. Ladder

4. Cross

5. Hamburger

Key Signal Words to Help Students Determine Text Patterns

Chronological Sequence:

before	after	afterward
during	following	then
meanwhile	preceding	initially
later	soon	immediately
first	next	when
finally	today	as soon as
now	not long after	

Description:

above	below	across
behind	in front of	in back of
beside	between	over
under	to the right/left	on top of
inside	outside	down

Comparison/Contrast:

both	but	yet
still	although	even though
compared with	different from	in common
as opposed to	as well as	though
on the other hand	similar to	similarly
otherwise	however	either ... or

Concept/Definition:

for instance	that is	thus
refers to	put another way	in other words
is characterized by		

www.ahaprocess.com

Generalization:

usually	furthermore	always
additionally	moreover	often
because of	clearly	generally
for example	not only ... but also	never
conclusively	in fact	typically

Cause/Effect:

effects of	because	in order to
therefore	for this reason	when ... then
consequently	accordingly	if ... then

Sorting with Pictures

Step sheet:
1. Look carefully at the picture.
2. Divide the picture into four quadrants.
3. On the card below, make a list of the things you see in each quadrant: people, items, climate, geography.
4. What is happening?
5. What is being said/felt?

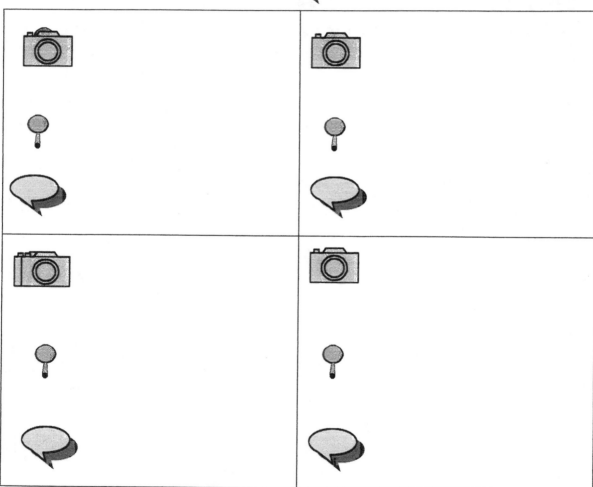

Why was the picture taken, drawing painted or sketched?
Does it reflect a point of view? _____

_____

Source: Connie Abernathy

Newspaper/Article Report

TOPIC: _____

WHO	WHAT	WHEN	WHY	HOW	WHERE

Write a paragraph using the information.

_____

_____

_____

_____

_____

_____

_____

Concept Diagram

Concept name: _____

Definition: _____
_____
_____

List the characteristics present in the concept:

ALWAYS PRESENT	SOMETIMES	NEVER

EXAMPLE	NON-EXAMPLE

Source: Marie Smith

Name: _____

Date: _____

TOPIC

Conclusion:

_____

_____

_____

_____

Reason	Reason	Reason

used w/propaganda/bias

Sequence/Process Chart

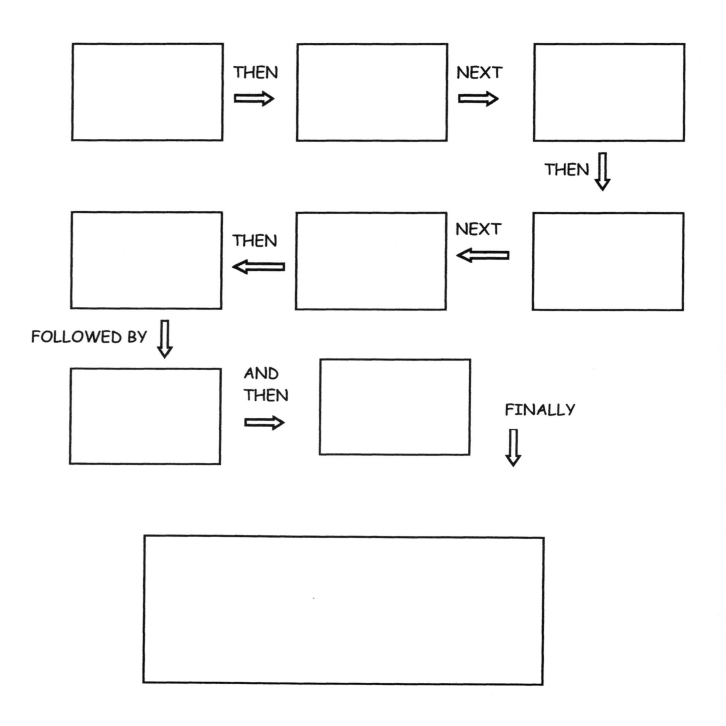

www.ahaprocess.com

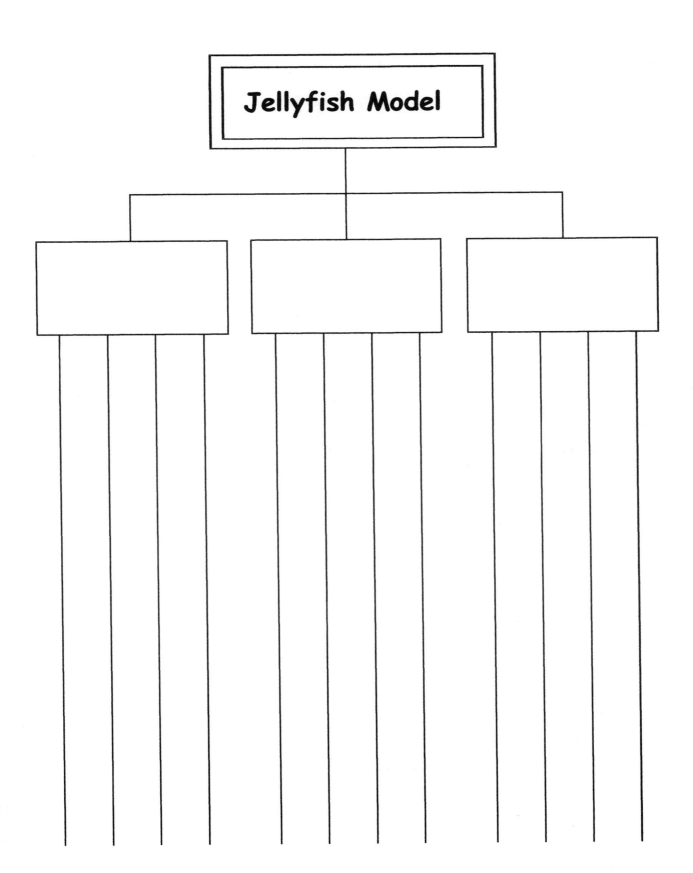

Test Tree

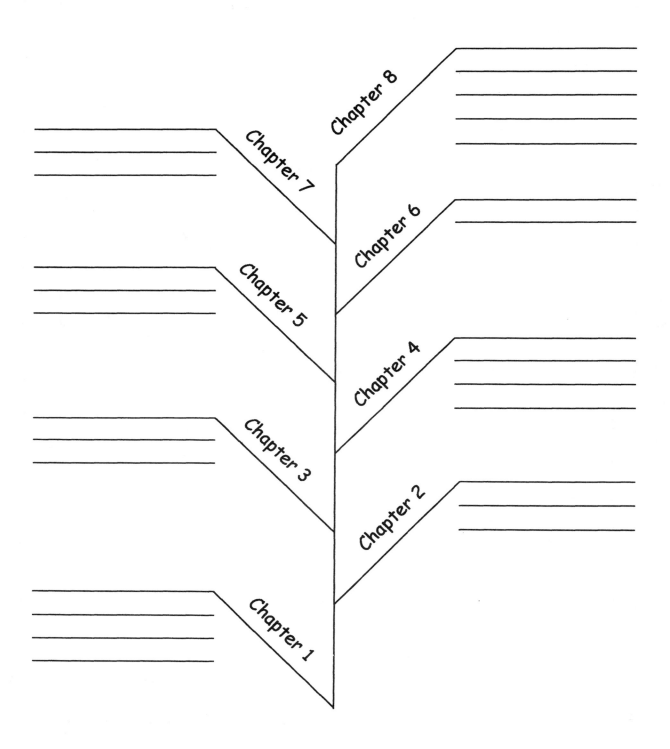

Chapter 8

Chapter 7

Chapter 6

Chapter 5

Chapter 4

Chapter 3

Chapter 2

Chapter 1

Research Folder

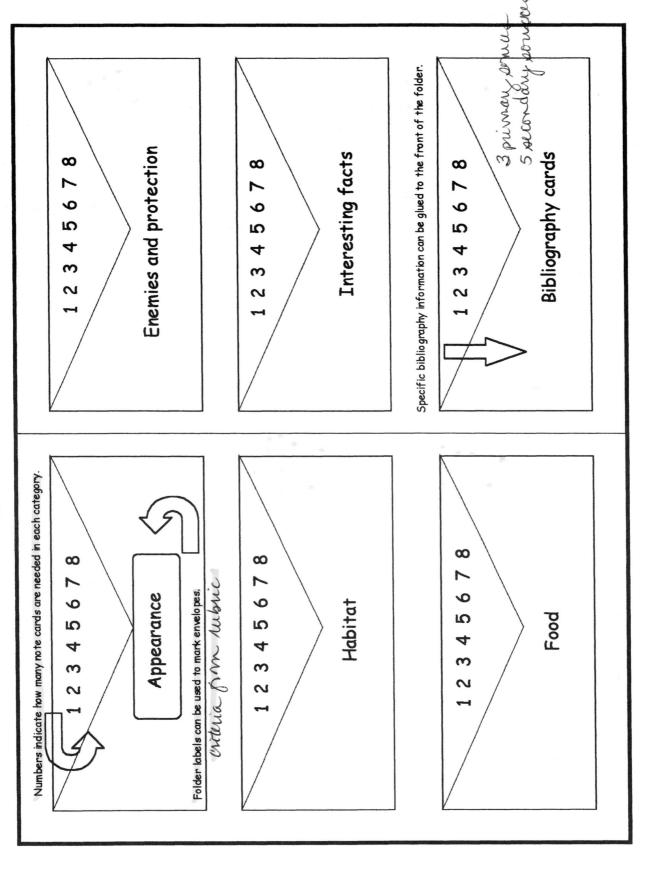

Numbers indicate how many note cards are needed in each category.

1 2 3 4 5 6 7 8

Appearance

Folder labels can be used to mark envelopes.
criteria from rubric

1 2 3 4 5 6 7 8

Habitat

1 2 3 4 5 6 7 8

Food

1 2 3 4 5 6 7 8

Enemies and protection

1 2 3 4 5 6 7 8

Interesting facts

Specific bibliography information can be glued to the front of the folder.

1 2 3 4 5 6 7 8

Bibliography cards

3 primary sources
5 secondary sources

Novel Folder

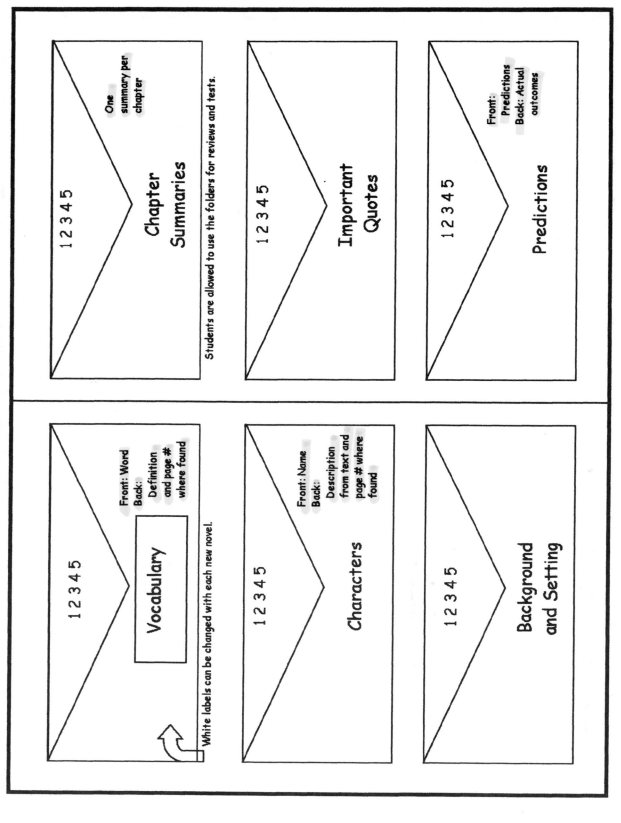

Chapter Summaries
1 2 3 4 5
One summary per chapter

Important Quotes
1 2 3 4 5

Predictions
1 2 3 4 5
Front: Predictions
Back: Actual outcomes

Vocabulary
1 2 3 4 5
Front: Word
Back: Definition and page # where found

Characters
1 2 3 4 5
Front: Name
Back: Description from text and page # where found

Background and Setting
1 2 3 4 5

Students are allowed to use the folders for reviews and tests.

White labels can be changed with each new novel.

Research Paper

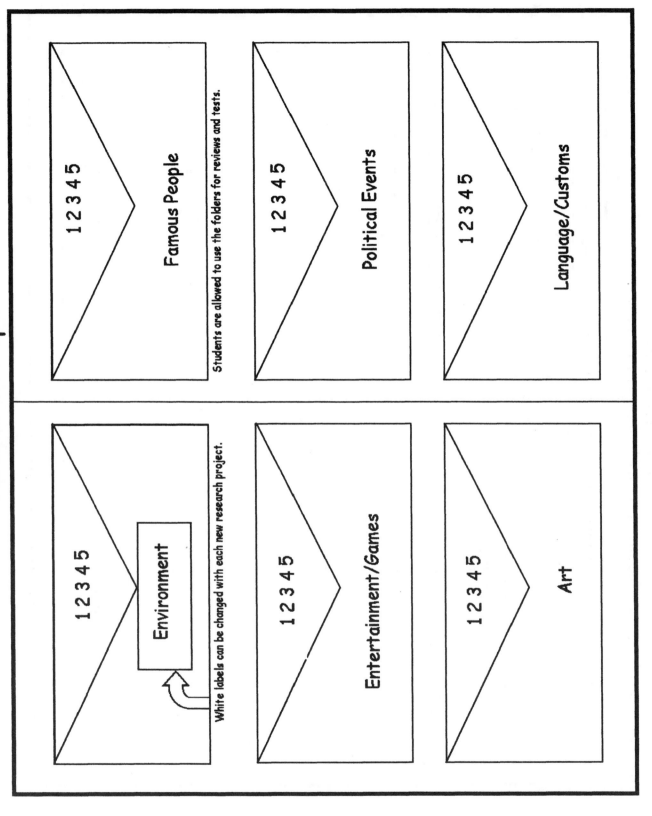

1 2 3 4 5 — Famous People

Students are allowed to use the folders for reviews and tests.

1 2 3 4 5 — Political Events

1 2 3 4 5 — Language/Customs

1 2 3 4 5 — Environment

White labels can be changed with each new research project.

1 2 3 4 5 — Entertainment/Games

1 2 3 4 5 — Art

Math Folder

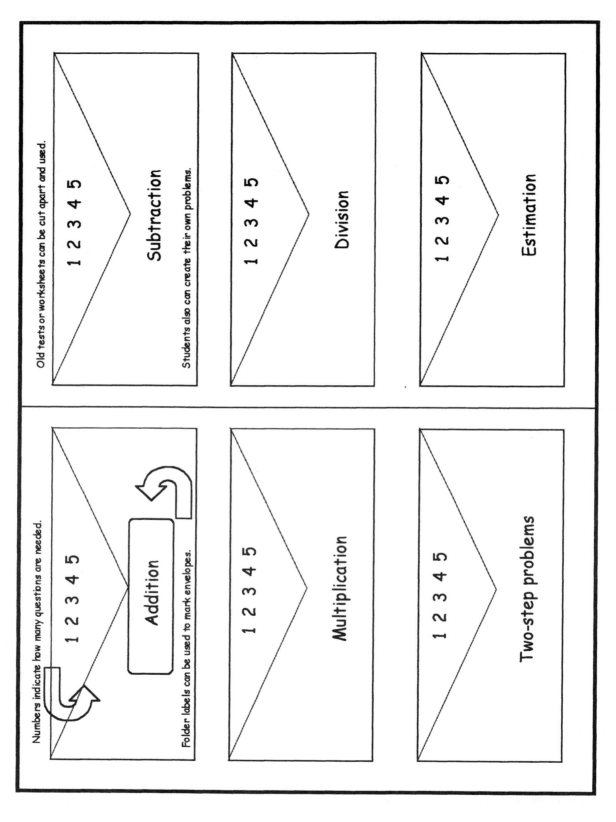

Numbers indicate how many questions are needed.

1 2 3 4 5

Addition

Folder label can be used to mark envelopes.

1 2 3 4 5

Multiplication

1 2 3 4 5

Two-step problems

Old tests or worksheets can be cut apart and used.

1 2 3 4 5

Subtraction

Students also can create their own problems.

1 2 3 4 5

Division

1 2 3 4 5

Estimation

166

Social Studies

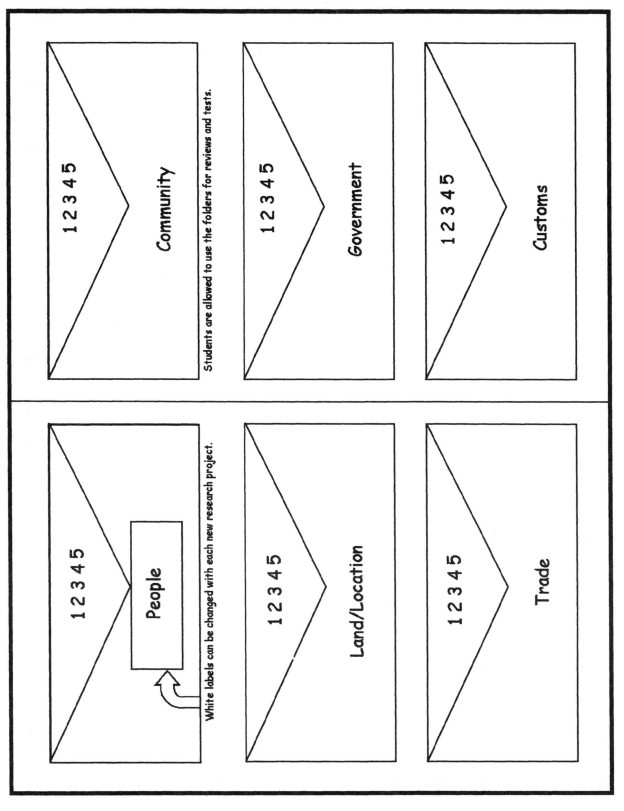

1 2 3 4 5

Community

1 2 3 4 5

Government

1 2 3 4 5

Customs

Students are allowed to use the folders for reviews and tests.

1 2 3 4 5

People

White labels can be changed with each new research project.

1 2 3 4 5

Land/Location

1 2 3 4 5

Trade

Science

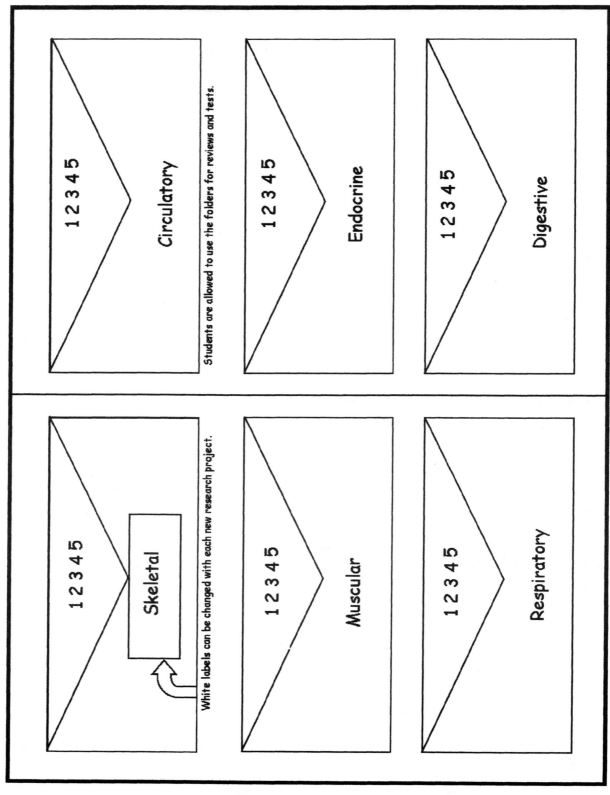

1 2 3 4 5

Circulatory

Students are allowed to use the folders for reviews and tests.

1 2 3 4 5

Endocrine

1 2 3 4 5

Digestive

1 2 3 4 5

Skeletal

White labels can be changed with each new research project.

1 2 3 4 5

Muscular

1 2 3 4 5

Respiratory

www.ahaprocess.com

Bibliography

Biemiller, Andrew. (2000). Vocabulary: the missing link between phonics and comprehension. *Perspectives,* Fall, 26-30.

Bloom, Benjamin. (1976). *Human Characteristics and School Learning.* New York, NY: McGraw-Hill Book Company.

Bransford, John D., Brown, Ann L., & Cocking, Rodney R. (Eds.). (1999). *How People Learn: Brain, Mind, Experience and School.* Washington, DC: National Academy Press.

Caine, Renate Nummela, & Caine, Geoffrey. (1997). *Education on the Edge of Possibility.* Alexandria, VA: Association for Supervision and Curriculum Development.

Enfield, Mary L., & Greene, Victoria. (1992). *Report Form Comprehensive Guide.* Bloomington, MN: Language Circle Enterprises.

Enfield, Mary L., & Greene, Victoria. (1992). *Story Form Comprehensive Guide.* Bloomington, MN: Language Circle Enterprises.

Enfield, Mary L., & Greene, Victoria. (1992). *Written Expression Kit.* Bloomington, MN: Language Circle Enterprises.

Feuerstein, Reuven, et al. (1980). *Instrumental Enrichment: An Intervention Program for Cognitive Modifiability.* Glenview, IL: Scott, Foresman & Co.

Feuerstein, Reuven, & Hoffman, Mildred. (1995). *Organization of Dots.* Palatine, IL: IRI/Skylight Publishing.

Feuerstein, Reuven. (1995). *Orientation of Space.* Palatine, IL: IRI/Skylight Publishing.

Goleman, Daniel. (1995). *Emotional Intelligence.* New York, NY: Bantam Books.

Greenspan, Stanley I., & Benderly, Beryl L. (1997). *The Growth of the Mind and the Endangered Origins of Intelligence.* Reading, MA: Perseus Books.

Jones, B.F., Pierce, J., & Hunter, B. (1988). Teaching students to construct graphic representations. *Educational Leadership,* 46 (4), 20-25.

Marzano, Robert J., & Arredondo, Daisy. (1986). *Tactics for Thinking.* Aurora, CO: Mid Continent Regional Educational Laboratory.

Munsch, Robert. (1983). *David's Father*. Toronto, Canada: Annick Press.

Payne, Ruby K. (1998). *A Framework for Understanding Poverty* (workbook). Highlands, TX: aha! Process.

Payne, Ruby K. (1998). *Learning Structures*. Highlands, TX: aha! Process.

Payne, Ruby K. (2002). *Understanding Learning*. Highlands, TX: aha! Process.

Resnick, Lauren B., & Klopfer, Leopold. (Eds.). (1989). *Toward the Thinking Curriculum: Current Cognitive Research*. Alexandria, VA: Association for Supervision and Curriculum Development, Publishers.

Rieber, Robert W. (Ed.). (1997). *The Collected Works of L.S. Vygotsky (Volume 4: The History of the Development of Higher Mental Functions)*. New York, NY: Plenum Press.

Sain, Judy, S. (2001). *Daily Math Practice for Virginia Standards of Learning (SOL) – Grade 4*. Highlands, TX: aha! Process.

Sharron, Howard, & Coulter, Martha. (1994). *Changing Children's Minds: Feuerstein's Revolution in the Teaching of Intelligence*. Exeter, United Kingdom: BPC Wheatons.

Shulman, Lee. (1987). Assessment for teaching: an initiative for the profession. *Phi Delta Kappan*, September, 38-44.

Skoglund, P., Lucas, M., Lucas, L., & Blaga, J. (1994). *ADD: Arithmetic Developed Daily*. Racine, WI: Grow Publications.

Stahl, Steven A. (1990). *Beyond the Instrumentalist Hypothesis: Some Relationships Between Word Meanings and Comprehension*. Champaign-Urbana, IL: University of Illinois at Champaign-Urbana Press.

Wong, Harry K., & Wong, Rosemary Tripi. (1998). *The First Day of School: How to Be an Effective Teacher* (Revised Edition). Mountainview, CA: Harry K. Wong, Publisher.

The I Know About Language/Writing Book. (1992). Alvin, TX: Devine Educational Corporation.

ORDER FORM

www.ahaprocess.com
PO Box 727, Highlands, TX 77562-0727
(800) 424-9484; fax: (281) 426-8705
store@ahaprocess.com

UPS SHIP TO ADDRESS: (no post office boxes, please)

NAME: _____ E-mail _____

ORGANIZATION: _____

ADDRESS: _____

CITY/STATE/ZIP: _____

TELEPHONE: _____ FAX: _____

QTY	TITLE	1-4 Copies	5+ Copies	Total
	A Framework for Understanding Poverty	22.00	15.00	
	Understanding Learning	10.00	7.00	
	A Framework for Understanding Poverty Workbook	7.00	7.00	
	Learning Structures Workbook	7.00	7.00	
	A Framework for Understanding Poverty Audio Workshop Kit (includes Day 1 & 2 audiotapes – 10 – and 4 books listed above) **S/H: $10.50**	225.00	225.00	
	Un Marco Para Entender La Pobreza	22.00	15.00	
	Putting the Pieces Together	7.00	7.00	
	Daily Math Practice for Virginia SOLs – Grade 4	22.00	15.00	
	Mr. Base Ten Invents Mathematics	22.00	15.00	
	Think Rather of Zebra	18.00	15.00	
	Berrytales – Plays in One Act	25.00	20.00	
	What Every Church Member Should Know About Poverty	22.00	15.00	
	A Picture Is Worth a Thousand Words	18.00	15.00	
	Bridges Out of Poverty: Strategies for Professionals & Communities	22.00	15.00	
	Removing the Mask: Giftedness in Poverty	25.00	20.00	
	Environmental Opportunity Profile (25/set-incl 1 FAQ)	25.00	25.00	
	Addit'l FAQs Environmental Opportunities Profile manual	3.00	3.00	
	Slocumb-Payne Teacher Perception Inventory (25/set)	25.00	25.00	
	Living on a Tightrope: a Survival Handbook for Principals	22.00	15.00	
	Hidden Rules of Class at Work	22.00	15.00	
	Tucker Signing Strategies Video & Manual **S/H: $8.50**	125.00	125.00	
	Tucker Signs Reference Cards on CD	25.00	25.00	
	Take-Home Books for Tucker Signing Strategies for Reading	22.00	15.00	
	Preventing School Violence – 5 videos & manual **S/H: $15.00**	995.00	995.00	
	Preventing School Violence CD – PowerPoint presentation	25.00	25.00	
	Preventing School Violence Training Manual	15.00	15.00	
	Audiotapes, What Every Church Member Should Know About Poverty	25.00	25.00	
	Meeting Standards & Raising Test Scores When You Don't Have Much Time or Money (4 videos/training manual **S/H: $15.00**	995.00	995.00	
	Meeting Standards & Raising Test Scores Training Manual	18.00	18.00	
	Meeting Standards & Raising Test Scores Resource Manual	18.00	18.00	
	Rita's Stories (2 videos) **S/H: $8.50**	150.00	150.00	
	Ruby Payne Video Sampler	10.00	10.00	
	aha! 12 oz. mugs (white with red logo and website)	8.00	2 @ 15.00	
	Rubygems! 16-month calendar – Ideas for working with parents **$2 S/H**	10.00	10.00	
For Certified Trainers Only – Please note date/city of training:				
	A Framework for Understanding Poverty Video Sets (12 videos) (Day 1 & Day 2 of Framework seminar) **S/H: $25.00**	1995.00	1995.00	
	Audiotapes, Training of Trainers	125.00	125.00	
	A Framework for Understanding Poverty CD – PowerPoint presentation	50.00	50.00	
	A Framework for Understanding Poverty CD – Enhanced PowerPoint pres.	100.00	100.00	
	Bridges Out of Poverty CD – PowerPoint presentation	50.00	50.00	

Total Quantity		Subtotal	
S/H: 1-4 books – $4.50 plus $2.00 each additional book up to 4 books, [1 calendar $2]		S/H	
5+ books – 8% of total, *(special S/H for videos).* E-mail for international rates.		Tax	
TAX: 8.25% Texas residents only. **Prices subject to change.**		**Total**	

AmEx   MC   Visa   Discover

CREDIT CARD # _____ EXP. DATE_____Signature_____

AUTHORIZATION # _____ PO # _____ (please fax PO with order) Check # _____

More eye-openers at ...

www.ahaprocess.com

- **Join our aha! News List!**

  Receive the latest income and poverty statistics *free* when you join! Then receive periodic news and updates, recent articles by Dr. Payne and more!

- **Register for Dr. Payne's U. S. National Tour**

- **Visit our on-line store**

    Books

    Videos

    Workshops

- **Learn about our Certified Trainer Programs**

    A Framework for Understanding Poverty

    Bridges Out of Poverty

    Meeting Standards & Raising Test Scores

- **Register for courses at our Training Center**